Paper Dance

OTHER PERSEA ANTHOLOGIES

Poets for Life: Seventy-Six Poets Respond to AIDS
Edited by Michael Klein

Things Shaped in Passing: More "Poets for Life"
Writing from the AIDS Pandemic
Edited by Michael Klein and Richard McCann

Imagining America: Stories from the Promised Land
Edited by Wesley Brown & Amy Ling

Visions of America:
Personal Narratives from the Promised Land
Edited by Wesley Brown & Amy Ling

America Street: A Multicultural Anthology of Stories
Edited by Anne Mazer

Going Where I'm Coming From:
Memoirs of American Youth
Edited by Anne Mazer

A Walk in My World:
International Short Stories About Youth
Edited by Anne Mazer

First Sightings: Contemporary Stories of American Youth
Edited by John Loughery

Into the Widening World:
International Coming-of-Age Stories
Edited by John Loughery

Show Me a Hero:
Great Contemporary Stories About Sports
Edited by Jeanne Schinto

Virtually Now:
Stories of Science, Technology, and the Future
Edited by Jeanne Schinto

Paper Dance

55 LATINO POETS

EDITED BY
VICTOR HERNÁNDEZ CRUZ
LEROY V. QUINTANA
AND VIRGIL SUAREZ

A Karen and Michael Braziller Book
PERSEA BOOKS/NEW YORK

for the children

Since this page cannot legibly accommodate all copyright notices, pages 237–242 constitute an extension of the copyright page.

Copyright © 1995 by Victor Hernández Cruz
Leroy V. Quintana, and Virgil Suarez.

Persea Books, Inc.
171 Madison Avenue
New York, New York 10016

Library of Congress Cataloging-in-Publication Data

Paper dance : 55 Latino poets / edited by Victor Hernández Cruz,
Leroy V. Quintana, and Virgil Suarez.
        p.   cm.
        ISBN 0-89255-201-8
1. American poetry—Hispanic American authors. 2. Hispanic
Americans—Poetry. I. Cruz, Victor Hernández, 1949–
II. Quintana, Leroy. III. Suarez, Virgil, 1962–
            PS591.H58P36   1994
811'.54080868—dc20   94-15586
                                                         CIP

Designed by Arden Reardon
Typeset in Trump Mediaeval by Keystrokes, Lenox, Massachusetts

Second Printing

Contents

Introduction

The idea for this book emerged out of a deep desire to see exist an anthology which would gather and collect all of the major Latino and Latina poets living and writing in the United States. Previous anthologies, though filled with powerful and unique voices, aimed to present and focus largely on Puerto Rican and Chicano poets. In *Paper Dance*, we have striven for an inclusive, representative work that brings together all the voices, emerging and established, from across the country and from many different groups. No other work like it exists at the present time.

The poets in *Paper Dance* have developed at the center of America in its broader continental spirit. Their poetry best reflects this time and this place we inhabit. Though it continues to suffer from marginalization, it is anything but marginal. Growing in the interior sequis of the poets' homes and cultural tempos, it is an organic poetry, full of history and the exchanges among people. It travels through time zones and up and down geographic stairs in sweeps of images and narratives. Most of the poems were written in English, with an occasional Spanish word here and there, reflecting a multilingualism that is perhaps less "new" and "unusual" that it would first seem. Like all poets, including William Carlos Williams who published a book with a Spanish title, *Al Que Quiere*, and Ezra Pound who used some twenty-two different languages in his *Cantos*, the poets collected here are interested in language and in the use of new and other sounds.

This gathering of tongues is truly distinctive of the Americas. The United States has been shaped by many different cultures, each speaking, thinking, and feeling in many different languages. We have made a quiet pact to use English in the public sphere, but we have also enriched our English by accepting and circulating words and phrases from the many cultures that make up the American tapestry. Contact among different languages creates tension, new thought patterns, synthesis of ideas, hybrid words.

This is what human culture is all about. At the point of the greatest mixing and contact, we collectively experience our greatest achievements, our greatest leaps of awareness. In the regions of the United States where there has been the greatest racial and cultural mixing, we have seen emerge the most exciting aspects of our culture—art, music, writing. Each individual component making up the stew, or *ajiaco*, remains strong—can gain in strength, due to the blending. After all, any single language has already been formed by the mixing of other languages and by the changes brought about by common usage. It is not surprising that good poets will continue to mix and experiment and that from this stew of language and experience some of the best contemporary poetry will surface.

The work included in *Paper Dance* is representative of the styles, language, rhythms, issues, and concerns of younger and older, new and established, male and female poets from diverse origins in the American heritage—Chicano, Puerto Rican, Cuban, Guatemalan, Ecuadoran, and Colombian. From the established, we will hear the well-known voices of Julia Alvarez, Jimmy Santiago Baca, Judith Ortiz Cofer, Martín Espada, Gustavo Pérez Firmat, Naomi Quiñonez, Alberto Alvaro Ríos, Gloria Vando, and Tino Villanueva, to name a few. And, of course, we are showcasing many emerging and exciting new voices like Sandra M. Castillo, Adrian Castro, Silvia Curbelo, Diana Rivera, Deborah Salazar, Gina Valdez, and E. J. Vega.

The poems are well crafted, chosen not only for original breath and composition, but because they speak directly of bicultural experience. This is a poetry vital to all human experience, for it is positioned precisely at the center of blending, conflicting, melting of cultures endlessly transforming. The poems focus on and are unified by the following themes and perspectives: the "Americanization" process, the struggle to define, redefine, and attain the American Dream; the use of cultural myths; language and memory; gender; religion and spirituality; rural versus urban (the barrio) life; ideals and values; the role of Latino and Latina poets; the question of universality and specificity.

It is the history of our nation, singing here through personal experience, a lyrical montage that is also a bridging of the private to the communal. The tropical *guayaba* growing out of snow-covered cement.

We suggest that the reader merge with the poets within at his or her own likings. The poets and their poems, though chosen carefully and placed in alphabetical order, don't necessarily have to be read that way. Plunge in at any place, get to know the poet, his or her poetry, read everything, feel the rhythms and the beats of this wonderful world of Latino and Latina poetry. Whether or not there is communication is the job of the reader, whoever you are out there, craving good poetry. You.

*   *   *

We would like to thank the poets for being so generous and helpful, and our families for their incredible patience and tolerance as this project developed, submission by submission, from idea to anthology. A heartfelt thanks goes to our editor Karen Braziller and to Persea Books for publishing this book.

Victor Hernández Cruz, Aguas Buenas, Puerto Rico

Leroy V. Quintana, San Diego, California

Virgil Suarez, Tallahassee, Florida

Paper Dance

Shame

I washed
my arms
scrubbed
my face

powdered
soap
fell from
my hands

but
my skin
only got
redder

I was
just
another
itching

brown
boy
getting
ready

for school

L.A. Prayer

April 1992

something
was wrong
when buses
didn't come

streets
were
no longer
streets

how easy
hands
became
weapons

blows
gunfire
rupturing
the night

the more
we run
the more
we burn

o god
show us
the way
lead us

spare us
from ever
turning into
walking

matches
amidst
so much
gasoline

JULIA ALVAREZ

Storm Windows

She climbed toward the sky
when we did windows,
while I stood by, her helper,
doing the humdrum groundwork,
carrying her sloppy buckets
back and forth to the spigot,
hosing the glasses down
under her supervision
up there on a ladder
she had forbidden me.

I wanted to mount that ladder,
rung by rung, look down
into the gaping mouths of buckets,
the part in her graying hair.
I wanted to rise, polishing into each pane
another section of the sky.
Then give a kick, unbuckling
her hands clasped about my ankles,
and sail up, beyond her reach,
her house, her grounds, her mothering.

Dusting

Each morning I wrote my name
on the dusty cabinet, then crossed
the dining table in script, scrawled
in capitals on the backs of chairs,
practicing signatures like scales

while Mother followed, squirting
linseed from a burping can
into a crumpled-up flannel.

She erased my fingerprints
from the bookshelf and rocker,
polished mirrors on the desk
scribbled with my alphabets.
My name was swallowed in the towel
with which she jeweled the table tops.
The grain surfaced in the oak
and the pine grew luminous.
But I refused with every mark
to be like her, anonymous.

Homecoming

When my cousin Carmen married, the guards
at her father's finca took the guests' bracelets
and wedding rings and put them in an armored truck
for safekeeping while wealthy, dark-skinned men,
their plump, white women and spoiled children
bathed in a river whose bottom had been cleaned
for the occasion. She was Uncle's only daughter,
and he wanted to show her husband's family,
a bewildered group of sunburnt Minnesotans,
that she was valued. He sat me at their table
to show off my English, and when he danced with me,
fondling my shoulder blades beneath my bridesmaid's gown
as if they were breasts, he found me skinny
but pretty at seventeen, and clever.
Come back from that cold place, Vermont, he said,
all this is yours! Over his shoulder
a dozen workmen hauled in a block of ice
to keep the champagne lukewarm and stole

6

glances at the wedding cake, a dollhouse duplicate
of the family rancho, the shutters marzipan,
the cobbles almonds. A maiden aunt housekept,
touching up whipped cream roses with a syringe
of eggwhites, rescuing the groom when the heat
melted his chocolate shoes into the frosting.
On too much rum Uncle led me across the dance floor,
dusted with talcum for easy gliding, a smell
of babies underfoot. He twirled me often,
excited by my pleas of dizziness, teasing me,
saying that my merengue had lost its Caribbean.
Above us, Chinese lanterns strung between posts
came on and one snapped off and rose
into a purple postcard sky.
A grandmother cried: The children all grow up too fast.
The Minnesotans finally broke loose and danced a
        Charleston
and were pronounced good gringos with latino hearts.
The little sister, freckled with a week of beach,
her hair as blonde as movie stars', was asked
by maids if they could touch her hair or skin,
and she backed off, until it was explained to her,
they meant no harm. This is all yours,
Uncle whispered, pressing himself into my dress.
The workmen costumed in their workclothes danced
a workman's jig. The maids went by with trays
of wedding bells and matchbooks monogrammed
with Dick's and Carmen's names. It would be years
before I took the courses that would change my mind
in schools paid for by sugar from the fields around us,
years before I could begin to comprehend
how one does not see the maids when they pass by . . . .
—It was too late, or early, to be wise—
The sun was coming up beyond the amber waves
of cane, the roosters crowed, the band struck up
Las Mananitas, a morning serenade. I had a vision
that I blamed on the champagne:
the fields around us were burning. At last

7

a yawning bride and groom got up and cut
the wedding cake, but everyone was full
of drink and eggs, roast pig, and rice and beans.
Except the maids and workmen,
sitting on stoops behind the sugar house,
ate with their fingers from their open palms
windows, shutters, walls, pillars, doors,
made from the cane they had cut in the fields.

JIMMY SANTIAGO BACA

---

from **Poem VI**

Cruising back from 7–11
esta mañana
in my '56 Chevy truckita,
beat up and rankled
farm truck,
clanking between rows
of new shiny cars—

> "Hey fella! Trees need pruning
> and the grass needs trimming!"

A man yelled down to me
from his 3rd-story balcony.

> "Sorry, I'm not the gardener,"
> I yelled up to him,

Funny how in the Valley
an old truck symbolizes prestige
and in the Heights, poverty.

Worth is determined in the Valley
by age and durability,
and in the Heights, by newness
and impression.

In the Valley,
the atmosphere is soft and worn,
things are shared and passed down.
In the Heights,
the air is blistered with the glaze
of new cars and new homes.

How many days of my life
I have spent fixing up
rusty broken things,
charging up old batteries,
wiring pieces of odds and ends together!
Ah, those lovely bricks
and sticks I found in fields
and took home with me
to make flower boxes!
The old cars I've worked on
endlessly giving them tune-ups,
changing tires, tracing
electrical shorts,
cursing when I've been stranded
between Laguna pueblo and Burque.
It's the process of making-do,
of the life I've lived between
breakdowns and break-ups, that has made life
worth living.

I could not bear a life
with everything perfect.

from **Poem XXIII**

Pancho, the barrio idiot.
Rumor is that una bruja from Bernalillo
le embrujo. Unshaven, chattering
and nodding to airy friends
that follow him,
he roams the barrio all day.
I see him at least twice a day—
walking on the ditch behind my house,
hours later walking across the bridge.

Harmless, la gente leave him alone
in his own fantasies,
to share his bread with invisible companions,
to speak back to voices
that brim over from his childhood memories.

I have seen him
on all fours in Raul's field
with the sheep. Or last Christmas
in the tree meowing like a cat.
You always fill my heart Pancho
with delight.

SANDRA M. CASTILLO

Leavings

They sleep in one large room:
Sonia, Tin, Zaida, Hectico, Roly.
And I cut through Peralta's backyard
to their tiny apartment, where at night
Hectico and I find our way to the roof
to count the stars.
Zaida is almost fifteen,
and Sonia and I take the bus downtown
every Sunday to collect discarded ice cream
cups to hold the pasta salad Sonia will make
for her birthday party.
Mother doesn't think we'll be able to go
to see her dance in her long, pink dress
as she smiles her way into womanhood.
Aunt Velia has called us to America.
Mother says that means I'll never again
sit on Sonia's tar-papered roof,
that Uncle Armando will move into our house,
and we'll be able to send gum in our letters
like Aunt Velia does now,
that the twins will learn English
before they remember these first
few years.

In dreams Aunt Velia waves,
signaling for us to come,
her tall body wrapped in an airmail
envelope, like a cloak.
Mother waves back, clutching the twins
in her arms, and begs me to hurry,
but I hesitate, knowing Sonia has had
a slow day.

Abuelo Leopoldo Sneaks a Bite of Cream Cheese

I don't think Mother believed me when I first said
it had not been me who left teeth prints
on the cream cheese Tio Berto got through la bolsa negra.
I remember she approached me twice,
and though I knew she asked because it was my habit
to overuse my adolescent teeth,
I grew scared because I thought it wasn't the cheese
that worried her and this was a mystery
we didn't need: we were suspicious enough.
Carmina and Abraham had just taken el comite
from Ebita's father and Mother was afraid
they knew Tio Berto knew where to get ham, milk, cheese,
and the Tia Estela had worked for Lima
in the '50s and had known Lima's people
had conspired against Batista and would imprison
them both. We were filling out forms,
taking passport pictures, waiting
for our number to come up, hoping our neighbors
wouldn't find out before we were ready to admit
we had been claimed. Mother was worried
one of the relatives would end up in Manga Larga,
La Granja, El Principe, Melena 1, Melena del Sur.
She was praying all our family would have a flight
out in los vuelos de la libertad and that none
of our secrets would spill in juicios populares,
permutas. And because Paulina was cleaning
our house on Saturdays, Mother approached her, too.
Though I am not sure what she said or how she said it.
It wasn't Paulina, I remember her saying,
her fear growing like Abuela Isabel's heart.

For El Niño on His Arrival in the United States

Though I never prayed for you as a child,
remember you only in mechanic shades of blue,
I would have recognized you anywhere;
you are Abuela Isabel, Tio Berto, Padrino Maurillio,
and Bisabuelo Enrique who died young.

Mother says that you grew up hearing the story
because Abuela didn't want you to forget
that Leopoldo, your father, my grandfather,
left you nameless by denying her the right
to name you, or any of her boy children,
that when she told him their first boy
would carry her dead father's name,
he told her he had already christened him
though he was not yet born.

Abuela never called you anything but "el niño,"
the baby, and you never responded to his call.

At sixty, you are still that small child
Abuela holds in pictures,
the only one who understood,
the only one whose son Enrique carries
Grandmother's wish.

Pulling the Muse from the Drum

We petitioned the four directions
asked that their brother thunder
their sister lightning
escort us on a stroll
around architecture of goatskin y wood
Escort us on a quest
to pull the muse from the drum

The relation between drum & tongue
was there
when the mythic word
heard its first dialogue
between seven thunder n' seven lightning
something about cedar
wanting the charm of speech
The union was there
when the first word
the first drum
imitated sighs from jungles
a repartee
witnessed by jubilant stars

*

When chiefs' princesses
were traded for spice & steel
chained & herded into Spanish galleons
How ominous to watch from a bush
sons of Felipe or Charles
iron vested men stalking
the Ivory Coast

*

Drums with thunder's spirit
embedded in wood
(ache olu bata)
had to stay
yet memory brought the word
the song
ache olu bata
there was a rebirth
of sound

Rhythms arrived hidden in a pageantry
of scars & piercings
Soon it was decreed
that no drummings/
toques de tambor
will be allowed
for it was a known fact
drums excited people
Masters did not want property
to rebel
drum became whisper of rebellion
tongue of freedom
so feared by Spain

*

Yet wood & goat skin
continued their speeches
discretely in Caribbean jungles
The language of hands hide & cedar
could not be silenced
the ancestors' mother tongue
thundering who they were
where they came from—

(Oruba iyalo ile mio)
was their muse
was their poem

*

We hear the sound of history
through stained walls in Little Havana
graffiti park in Lower East Side
frozen lake Wicker Park Chitown
grooved into people's struts
It is you
It is me
is we
unidos Latinos
A collection of feathered drums
red & White
repiqueando
We pulling the muse
from the drum
the muse that is we

Herald of Cocos (I)

for Victor Hernández Cruz

The breath of jesters
the tongues of queens.
There are moments England
loses rhythm
& borrows legs from Africa
arms from Flamenco
a sonorous Taino echo
of canoa/canoe.
There are moments in American midnights
this occurs on the lower west side

the upper east side
of the Atlantic.

We summon from the sound of fruits
the aura of congas dripping a pulse
a display of cultural feathers
peacocks with ebony sheaths
ivory handles
ruby blades cutting
through chants of ignorance.
We are a beyond generation
bereft of echoes.
Antennas with eyes of rainbow
walking towards a point
just past the horizon
choosing the language
will ignite
ready to fuel a generation of rainbows
arriving on plumed serpents.

The heat & humidity licks
the comfort from our skin.
Cities/barrios where la raza
is running
la raza escaping
the cold talcum powder falling
the sky is talking
dreams of migration
from tropical forestation
from islands vestid(o) in green
to islands of electric(o) steel—
who is Cuba fleeing
where is Santo Domingo drifting
why is Puerto Rico sailing.
Aqui is the steel that is frozen.
Alla is green that can't be forgotten.

Through cities swimming in neon
crowds swaying like accordions
a tango of speech
many lips spell the message
in Lower East Side with pachangas
in Little Havana with guayaberas
in the Mission with Tolteca chancletas—
la raza has not melted
we are a beyond generation
walking towards a point
just past el horizonte.

Morning Geography

Suppose the flower rioting on my desk, an exotic shout of
    yellow
streaked with red and ruffled like an agitated jungle bird,

suppose this flower, large as my hand, could be pulled apart
and the sweetness wrung out the way we did honeysuckle
    so long

ago on heavy summer nights with fireflies: *This drop of*
    honey
for courage, this drop of honey for love, this drop for
    anything

you are dreaming of . . . Last night I dreamed a woman I love
(in Spanish we say *dreamed* with, *soñe* con *Noemi*) running
    furiously

through Texas sagebrush to save her Uncle Mohammed,
    who died
on a mountain in Palestine years ago, a hermit who wanted
    no saving.

Dreams are like this, make all things possible. The way just
    now,
still drugged with sleep, I supposed a loud flower could save
    us, tell us

something about sweetness when half a world away a man
    tends a fire
in the street before his tiny rug shop, a short distance from
    some broken

buildings. He breathes the dense smoke of burning rubber, tires
to make the bombers think they've already struck here.
    Suppose we could

have coffee with him, strong, laced with cardamom and
    small talk.
Suppose we'd figured out, on those immense lost summer
    nights

or any other nights, or days, how to get at the sweetness
without tearing the proud throat of even one blossom.

Women Talk of Flowers at Dusk

Some things can only be spoken in the dark, you'd say each
    time you told about Dolores,
a name that means *pain*. We'd sit in dimming light at the
    chipped kitchen table where the past

showed in layers of old paint: exile from *México*, your forced
    marriage, the Great Depression.
You with a cigarette and a shot of *Paul Jones*, a brittle voice,
    telling how your mother died

in the half light of cheap rented rooms in the Turks' *barrio*.
    She was a nurse who recognized
the blood she coughed, but called it *roses* to ease your fears.
    Huacha was twelve and you, ten.

Even then you led. You hid in the jacaranda and, fierce with
    tears, barred your grandfather
when he arrived too late in his fancy carriage and fine frock
    coat. *Usted no tiene porqué*

estar aquí. No right to come here. You would always despise
   the jacaranda. *Mi madre muerta.*
Muerta. Y él! He calmly sent for pins to hold the sheet tight
   to the body. The first Indian doctor

in *Mérida*, he'd raised his daughter to be a lady, not his fault
   she'd come to this. He wouldn't look
at her wasted corpse, the flowers framing her face, the
   borrowed crucifix. She'd refused to stay

well-married, would not respect his choice and turn a deaf
   ear, blind eye, the other cheek
to a husband cajoling conquests behind palm fans, his seed
   spent in every street. Instead,

she'd made her own life in this damp *barrio*, nursing a
   company of women, the poor,
everything her father struggled to forget. The funeral wagon
   stopped at the corner, too wide

for the narrow alley. You, your sister, some Indian women,
   wept at the gate. Only men
were allowed at the grave, but he wouldn't go. Yet he
   couldn't escape the wild marigold

that fell from her temple as they hoised her onto the
   pauper's dray. That sight was a slap,
Grandmother, that stung his face then and every time you
   told the story. Even now the flame

of that marigold is in me, you gone these fifteen years,
   Dolores almost a century. So, too,
it's come to me to heal the roses in the blood, a need to let go
   of the sins of the fathers,

open the dark vaults of the heart. Let me begin here, in lives
   that are and are not my own,
to forgive even the jacaranda that blooms and blooms
   without mercy.

The Poet Is Served Her Papers

So tell me about fever dreams,
about the bad checks
we scrawl with our mouths,
about destiny missing
last bus to oblivion.
I want to tell lies
to the world and believe it.
Speak easy, speak
spoken to, speak lips
opening on a bed of nails.
Hear the creaking of cardboard
in these telling shoes?
The mint of my mind
gaping far out of style?
Hear the milling
of angels on the head
of a flea? My broke blood
is sorrel, is a lone
mare, is cashing in
her buffalo chips.
As we come to the cul-de-sac
of our heart's slow division
tell me again about true
love's bouquet, paint hummingbird
hearts taped to my page.
Sign me over
with xxx's and "passion."
Seal on the lick
of a phone—
my life. And pay.
And pay. And pay.

Blue Full Moon in Witch

I come to you on an angel's moon,
when heat off foam rises to a crest,
on sheets of stainless sea, on
shallowed ice on shattered diamond leis,
where above it all an arctic cauldron lies
and covers us in woven halo gems.
Spring still forms and shudders crystals.
Since before the hail there is this ring.
Before the rest there is this missing
fractured light in the captioned
reruns of our dreams. I want you
and my heart still licks
its heaven. I want you
and heaven pulls its ring.

From the Cables of Genocide

Who gave you permission to detonate
this neutron bomb in my heart?
My imploding senses reel
in the leftover scent of you,
squirrel, plural wrecker, acorn
masher. My laurel leaves
wither to ash, the clot
of my rose, a dirt devil
in the branches of my veins.
Proven destination, where are you
now? Does the blood still flow
camellias like a slap when I see you
crossing my backyards, the alleys
where we met, where we kissed
red stars? Moon of my moon,
let me wish you. Let April

catch in the throat of our beating
white flags. Let me not be
the only fool standing.
The only gas breathed
is you.

JUDITH ORTIZ COFER

The Latin Deli: An Ars Poetica

Presiding over a formica counter,
plastic Mother and Child magnetized
to the top of an ancient register,
the heady mix of smells from the open bins
of dried codfish, the green plantains
hanging in stalks like votive offerings,
she is the Patroness of Exiles,
a woman of no-age who was never pretty,
who spends her days selling canned memories
while listening to the Puerto Ricans complain
that it would be cheaper to fly to San Juan
than to buy a pound of Bustelo coffee here,
and to Cubans perfecting their speech
of a "glorious return" to Havana—where no one
has been allowed to die and nothing to change until then;
to Mexicans who pass through, talking lyrically
of *dolares* to be made in El Norte—
all wanting the comfort
of spoken Spanish, to gaze upon the family portrait
of her plain wide face, her ample bosom
resting on her plump arms, her look of maternal interest
as they speak to her and each other
of their dreams and their disillusions—
how she smiles understanding,
when they walk down the narrow aisles of her store
reading the labels of packages aloud, as if
they were the names of lost lovers: *Suspiros,
Merengues,* the stale candy of everyone's childhood.

She spends her days
slicing *jamon y queso* and wrapping it in wax paper

tied with string: plain ham and cheese
that would cost less at the A&P, but it would not satisfy
the hunger of the fragile old man lost in the folds
of his winter coat, who brings her lists of items
that he reads to her like poetry, or the others,
whose needs she must divine, conjuring up products
from places that now exist only in their hearts—
closed ports she must trade with.

The Medium's Burden

In the morning kitchens of my friends,
I must gather the dreams they spill
like bread crumbs on the table.
Over coffee and easy talk, I see
their lives swirling in my cup.

Virginia's restless night
yields an old woman in rags,
Medusa eyes turning everything
to stone: her husband frozen on their bed
against the wall, the baby
in his crib becomes a statue of Cupid,
even the dog, a bark stuck in his throat,
is petrified at the door.

Cristina is buried alive, tucked into the grave
by loved ones. She claims a sense of peace
in her coffin, where she sleeps deeply
under the thick, warm comforter of earth.

They must ask me what it means, and I
must say. Either way, speech or silence,
means I have stayed beyond my welcome.

In my own recurring dream,
I am the woman in the painting
whose mouth is sealed in a smile
beneath the pentimento, whose eyes
break through the canvas to watch
the anonymous crowds drift by,
throwing me their casual glances
like alms in a cup. I know their hearts,
and I am tormented forever
by knowing.

My Grandfather's Hat

in memory of Basiliso Morot Cordero

I cannot stop thinking of that old hat
he is wearing in the grave: the last gift
of love from his wife before they fell
into the habit of silence.

Forgotten as the daughters chose
the funeral clothes, it sat
on his dresser as it always had:
old leather, aromatic of his individual self,
pliable as an old companion, ready to go
anywhere with him.

The youngest grandchild remembered
and ran after her father, who was carrying
the old man's vanilla suit—the one worn to bodas,
bautismos, and elections—like a lifeless
child in his arms: *No te olvides
del sombrero de abuelo.*

I had seen him hold the old hat in his lap
and caress it as he talked of the good times,

and when he walked outside, place it on his head
like a blessing.

My grandfather, who believed in God,
the Gracious Host, Proprietor of the Largest Hacienda.
May it be so. May heaven
be an island in the sun,
where a good man may wear his hat with pride,
glad that he could take it with him.

Lucha Corpi

On Being Alone: Berkeley, 1969

To Beatriz Pesquera

Between my eyes and the moon
there were
365 nights of insomnia,

a small crack in my stomach,

the pain of knowing he was not mine,

the ray of light from a star,

a band of wakeful raccoons
    looting the garbage cans of their treasure,

and my neighbor
    who ran
    crazed
    at midnight
    with nothing
    to shelter him
    from the full moon
    but a pair of torn socks
    and a straightjacket.

Translated by Catherine Rodríguez-Nieto

Rehearsals for the Wreck

To Berta, Ramona and Carolina

Other than the purple dreams of bougainvillea
and that crazy kitchen
I'd painted orange and electric blue
—colors I'd thought might please
the husband whose memory of me was already fading—
no joy at all was left behind
in that little house on 66th Street.

I left behind
like rehearsals for the wreck
the nights of held-back rage
and, amid cigarette butts and bottles,
the mornings of fragile sanity.

I took away with me
family photos,
my son and all his smiles,
little cans of oregano, saffron and basil,
and the boxes of salt and oats
I'd inherited from
so many of the friends and companions
who'd passed through my life:

the essence that nourishes this poem
as it drifts toward the sidewalk in an autumn
full of springtime

Translated by Catherine Rodríguez-Nieto

VICTOR HERNÁNDEZ CRUZ

---

from **Mesa Blanca**

If a kiss left the mental dimension,
Entering the bone of dance hall,
My ears would reclaim the sound
Of your intended love.

Mostly it would be lost.
Both the poetry and the music
But to this side of things only,
Cause flashing in the joy
Is the lord of the station,
So immediate as to almost
Be your tongue,
The salivic pointed,
When it truths together,
That moment when decisions are over,
And the motion is the only thought
Accomplished I hear the buttons
Slipping through the grooves of
Your finger tips
Out through the ether of the
Hole slice,
Now the back opens
As onto a land
Curving into a cave,
Most a moist is there—
That even fries darkness
Which when the language dissolves
Gets hot enough to eat.
And it is always like this.
And it is only like this.
Ah Ha.

Mesa Blanca

If I were writing on rock,
It would be the wind of the year
That caressing me will make
Me aware of the shadows on
A distant stone—
That signifies an eclipse
On some unseen roof,
From where in the form of
A kite a diamond leaves for heaven.

It would be that letter that I would
Make into a face
Let's say at the banquet of those,
who having been amazed at the arrival
Of boats
Punctuate on a key,
But for what door?

The sea a rush of miots,
Things like trousers have come out
Of there,
And bacalao which here has been
Fricasseed with calabasa,
So we have to church the word
Mestizo, Mezo
Half and Half—
So that text books claiming total
Taino vanishment
Should tour pages later erase
The word burundangala—
The sensational things coming together,
Of the Arowakian-Taino
The only thing that remains is
What is not gone:
The looks,
The gestures,

The thoughts,
The dreams,
The intuitions,
The memories,
The names of fruits,
Rivers,
The names of towns,
Vegetables,
Certain fish,
The gourd making music
In the mountain,
The maraca making feet
Areyto dance,
And this cigar between my fingers.

This is not to disagree with the
Anthropologist of text.
But merely to reaffirm what they mean
When they don't say.

This paper which was a tree
Is crying for its leaves,
That's the route of your mind
To dance its branches,
For that canopy red flower
Of the Floridas,
So high up in air spirit,
Flowing right through that bark,
A water shaft,
An urban lavender of bamboos
A city of juice composing,
Hidden apartments for that
Night frog,
To sing without rest
Till the roosters brush their
Beaks with the first
Arriving morning light.

The joyful noise of the night,
What might be coming from lips,
Or the rubbing of legs,
The full harmonic tropical berserk
Begging for love
In abundance
Not one thousand
But one thousand and one
Lights of cucubanos,
Morse coding lovers,
That come down,
Meow not now
of the cats—
For that's the flavor,
Within the opening of the
Two mountains,
A glance following the
River
That goes to fish its memories,
Scratched one next to the other
Like the grooves of shells,
The mountains that gave me life,
The city I had to fight.

To think that now no one believes
We were here.
The past in the smoke of the cigar,
Bringing the future in-formation.

Time Zones

Time is crying upon the backs of lizards,
Through the white of the medieval city
They dash,
The houses that are walking up the stairs,

Flowers out of ruins,
Further into the fortress,
The sounds of a language registers
In our dreams,

Words which are my hat in the city,
Coming through the bamboo
The shadows of lost meaning—
Tilted light making slivers
Through the forest of the mambo
Behind the eyes,

Time will shine your head into skull
The circle song will come again and again,
If we forget how to lay out a village,
Just open a guayava in half,
These seeds are perfect,
And can guide you back,
Your hands the electric of the ghosts,

In the Persia shining of guitars,
A belly button silks upon a horse,
Enters a tent of rhythms,
Makes the trees dance into shape,
Ruben Dario saw them in the river,
Bathing in the echoes of the castles,
His Indio head,
Clean enough to measure
The tempo of a camel,
The first string that vibrated
The Rock of Gibraltar,
To sway greco-roman lips,
Arising fire of Gypsy song,
Was making castile dress and un-dress,
With the sounds that were hitting the moon
And falling down unto earth as colors.

Of boats that were my shoes,
Atlantic cha cha cha,
Splicing through 101st Street brick,
Which covered dancing verdure green
Rectangular mangoes,
Cylindric bananas
Sounds in the sky blue tropic: mind.

Trees are making maracas
That will soon make you dance,

Water is their god of cadence,
As I sea walk through coconut heights,
Legs of tamarind,
Purple orchids arranged like syllables,
Insects of the morning dew sting verses on cafe.
In embroidery of Italians,
Garcilaso came to Jose Marti,
Who ducked Spanish spies
In Manhattan
And hugged Walt Whitman's beard in Philadelphia
As the Cuban Habaneras shango
Made it south to Tango.

Boats are ages sailing on the water,
Parrots are flying out of castanets,
Flamenco peeling pineapples
That go up the river,
The water that became Vilmikis language,
As a cane field disappears into a bottle,
To awake in a little town
With molasses orbiting the cathedral,
A wooden saint slicing through the
Mountain full of potassium radiation,
Slanted platanos pointing into medieval
Liturgy,
Bongo and ocean waves carving
Fantasmal antiquity

Through the fabulous language
That has taken the shape of
An Andalusian rhyming door,
One after the other.
Perfume pagano
Sailing out of the archways,
As Ricardo Ray turns into a centipede,
Marching across a Brooklyn piano,

For dancers to Sanskrit their
Gypsy feet,
Upon Baghdad ceramic tile,
Caribbean sun melts the caramel,
Making our first national flag:
White skirts waving in the air.

Machetes taking off like helicopters
Chopping off branches for timbale sticks,
The hands of the sun hitting the
Moon like a drum—
Making the atmosphere of moisture
Heat up,
For the chorus of the song
To come back down polleniando
The carnival flower,
A serenade walkilipiando.

Sliding upon sea-shells,
That disappear into foam of time,
One age living next to another,
We are both things at once,
We are the cadaver that is
About to be born.

SILVIA CURBELO

Photograph from Berlin

Memory is the land standing still
for a moment, then a wave covers it.

Snapshots are shields—
what we remember in some way protects us.

In this particular one you're standing
on the balcony of your mother's house
waving at the soldiers passing through.

One of them, a handsome blond,
has caught your eye as he climbs
onto his friends' shoulders
to offer you something, some bread
or a piece of fruit,

his lieutenant's cap
poised over his heart
in a delicate cartoon of love.

Behind you the sky seems to float in all
directions, but the light holds
everything in place.

You cannot know how your life
will measure up against this moment,
your arm frozen in midair.

Your white handkerchief is like a wish.

Summer Storm

The waitress props open her book
against the sugar bowl
but doesn't read it.
She hums along with the hard rock station,
a song about a brittle love
and a piece of someone's heart.

Like a face behind a drawn shade
it has nothing to do with him.
She pours his coffee,
she will do that much.

He stares at his hands,
the coffee cup, the door,
saying nothing. She is beautiful.
When she shakes out her hair
he thinks of water spilling out
or the last moonlight shaking itself
out of the trees.

Could that be thunder
in the distance
or just the music rattling
in his ears? Anyway
he's stopped listening,
even to the radio.

Even the weather station
means nothing to him now.
He knows to sit still
and wait for thunder.
He's got time on his hands.
A good rain is worth a hundred years.

She stares out the plate glass windows.
Pinpoints of light

from the next town are blinking on.
He'll look at her now and then,
but not all of her,
a sleeve, a breast,
a glimpse of hair,
long like the longest night.

Witness

Someone will be there on that last turn,
someone will drive down that long road
for no reason
or pause in the parking lot of the next motel
holding the cold cup of coffee in his hands.
Call it the law of the land,
the only reason for going anywhere
is motion
because nothing ends and nothing
truly begins, the sky and the sea
are interchangeable and in another town
someone will punch up the headlights
with a used up lottery ticket in her hand.
What's the use of standing still
when everything we want keeps going
and whatever was hovers beneath our lives
like photo captions in a magazine?
This is the ocean and what crawled
out of it ten million years ago,
this is the road to Oz, and this
the dulled knife of regret.
And someone will always kick the front door open,
and someone will always lean against
that wall of light, the hook and bait
of wandering like another mouth to feed,
because nothing truly ends and nothing begins,

evolution is the wrong number
that connects, is the next face reflected
in the pool of history, the water
we are all baptized in,
and someone will always drive down
that long road for no reason or turn her eyes
towards the absolute certainty of space
knowing belief is one more accident of hope.
And what use is faith,
and what use some half-filled cup
when everyone will have to drink?

Martín Espada

The Lover of a Subversive Is Also a Subversive

The lover of a subversive
is also a subversive.
The painter's compañero was a conspirator,
revolutionary convicted
to haunt the catacombs of federal prison
for the next half century.
When she painted her canvas
on the beach, the FBI man
squatted behind her
on the sand, muddying his dark gray suit
and kissing his walkie-talkie,
a pallbearer who missed
the funeral train.

The painter who paints a subversive
is also a subversive.
In her portrait of him, she imagines
his long black twist of hair. In her portraits
of herself, she wears a mask
or has no mouth. She must sell the canvases,
for the FBI man ministered solemnly
to the principal at the school
where she once taught.

The woman who grieves for a subversive
is also a subversive.
The FBI man is a pale-skinned apparition
staring in the market.
She could reach for him
and only touch a pillar of ash
where the dark gray suit had been.

If she hungers to touch her lover,
she must brush her fingers
on moist canvas.

The lover of a subversive
is also a subversive.
When the beach chilled cold,
and the bright stumble of tourists
deserted, she and the FBI man
were left alone with their spying glances,
as he waited calmly
for the sobbing to begin,
and she refused to sob.

Coca-Cola and Coco Frío

On his first visit to Puerto Rico,
island of family folklore,
the fat boy wandered
from table to table
with his mouth open.
At every table, some great-aunt
would steer him with cool spotted hands
to a glass of Coca-Cola.
One even sang to him, in all the English
she could remember, a Coca-Cola jingle
from the forties. He drank obediently, though
he was bored with this potion, familiar
from soda fountains in Brooklyn.

Then, at a roadside stand off the beach, the fat boy
opened his mouth to coco frío, a coconut
chilled, then scalped by a machete
so that a straw could inhale the clear milk.
The boy tilted the green shell overhead

and drooled coconut milk down his chin;
suddenly, Puerto Rico was not Coca-Cola
or Brooklyn, and neither was he.

For years afterward, the boy marveled at an island
where the people drank Coca-Cola
and sang jingles from World War II
in a language they did not speak,
while so many coconuts in the trees
sagged heavy with milk, swollen
and unsuckled.

La Tumba de Buenaventura Roig

for my great-grandfather, died 1941

Buenaventura Roig,
once peasants in the thousands
streamed down hillsides
to witness the great eclipse
of your funeral.
Now your bones have drifted
with the tide of steep grass,
sunken in the chaos of weeds
bent and suffering
like canecutters in the sun.
The drunken caretaker
cannot find the grave,
squinting at your name,
spitting as he stumbles
between the white Christs
with hands raised
sowing their field
of white crosses.

Buenaventura Roig,
in Utuado you built the stone bridge
crushed years later by a river
raving like a forgotten god;
here sweat streaked your face
with the soil of coffee,
the ground where your nephew slept
while rain ruined the family crop,
and his blood flowered like flamboyán
on the white suit of his suicide.

Buenaventura Roig,
in the town plaza where you were mayor,
where there once was a bench
with the family name,
you shouted subversion
against occupation armies and sugarcane-patrones
to the jíbaros who swayed
in their bristling dry thicket of straw hats,
who knew bundles and sacks
loaded on the fly-bitten beast
of a man's back.

Buenaventura Roig,
not enough money for a white Christ,
lost now even to the oldest gravedigger,
the one with an English name
descended from the pirates of the coast,
who grabs for a shirt-pocket cigarette
as he remembers your funeral,
a caravan trailing in the distance
of the many years
that cracked the skin around his eyes.

Buenaventura Roig,
we are small among mountains,
and we listen for your voice
in the peasant chorus of five centuries,

waiting for the cloudburst of wild sacred song,
pouring over the crypt-wreckage of graveyard,
over the plaza and the church
where the statue of San Miguel
still chokes the devil with a chain.

Who Is Going to Tell Me?

For España

España, golden father of my ancestors,
who captured my mother as slave, stripped her naked,
plowed treasures from her shores.

To you, who claim hills most green, wine most sweet,
Spanish most precise, devotion most fervent.
Whose structured guitar the most elegant
and flamenco the most graceful.

To you, initiate
whose model blessed/cursed this western land
where Columbus recovered his wealthy Caribbean key
opening door to Española—Santo Domingo,
giving birth to the history of a million shames,
where the names of kings, imamus, caciques and warlords
were secrets disguised, abolished,
dissolved into myriads of bloodlines,
claiming invisible records, unwritten,
stolen from the luscious continents.

To you, father of my father,
whose table graced our tobacco fields,
whose whip increased the abundance of our sweet cane,
grinding sweat from roots to water your rose garden of
    thorns.
Whose court inspired our danzón, corrido, and gracious
    bomba,
giving rise to a new African drumbeat—the flight of the ball
    and chain,

creating the formulation of new words, esclavo, cimarrón,
    slave, rebel.

To you, who hide in mountains of golden courtly seals
inside handwrought manuscripts from the age of Ferdinand.
On whose gilded pages are inscribed
the names of my great grandmothers?
Inside what illustrations are located
the landmark homes of my great grandfathers?
On the maps of which islands
rest their simple graves where I may pay homage to my
    ancestors?
In whose kingly court
did my great grand-aunt wet nurse the master's brats?
Perhaps a future uncle, or slightly remembered landowner.
And which of my grand cousins were teachers?
Masters of their craft, respected noblemen, and women of
    wisdom?
In whose library will I find their books? Tales of their lives?
On which ships did my captured relatives sail?
At which ports did their feet first land?
To which continents were relatives dispersed?
To Brazil, Venezuela, Argentina, Bolivia,
Colombia, Costa Rica, Cuba, Ecuador,
Peru, the Dominican Republic, Uruguay, Jamaica,
Haiti, the Caribbean Antilles, the Mexican Coast, Panamá,
Yucatan, the thirteen colonies, New Orleans, Virginia,
South Carolina, Mississippi, Alabama, Nueva York?
To you, singing canticles of Spanish kings of Barcelona,
where Maximillian danced his Roman feast of world
    conquest,
forming the anguished tears of Goya,
forging the broken cubes of Picasso,
giving substance to the cries of García Lorca.

In all your illustrious bounty hides a legacy denied.
Yet, not one line of testimony to this truth of shame,

nor one admission of guilt, nor humble apology,
nor effort to replace what was defiled, dismembered.

To you, España, prize of Europe,
host to the colonized West,
solicitor of rich ports,
seducer of saintly Indians,
golden father of my ancestors, who captured my mother as
        slave,
stripped her naked, plowed treasures from her shores.

I want to know your future.

What new paintings will be created on whose walls?
Whose names will emerge in which new brilliant journals?
What melodies will evolve from our mixing?
In whose gardens will we water our visions?

I want to know
who will decide our fate?
You, or I, or WE together?
Will I be free to discover my own path?
Uncover a new journey no one else has known?
Designing my life spaces in my own natural colors,
tropical parades of evergreens,
caribbean blue seas, sand surfaces,
and mountain-rain-banana-leaf horizons.

I want to know.

Who is going to tell me?

Oshun's Love Poem

The first time I saw you on the mountain,
scouting through the luscious forest,
hunting with your golden bow
erect towards heaven.
Brush full, blue sky and yellow paint
across your warrior face,
your hunter's fierce stare, obsessed
like a mad priest.
I watched you visible like sunlight
that flows through the pattern of the trees,
two seconds before I fell
to the power of your silent arrow,
unsuspecting and wounded,
unable to disengage the snare
or break that heavy chain
locking my soul to yours,
as you held me tight and secure,
hand and feet tied limp across your back,
cross wrapped over your arm,
helpless against the curve of your neck,
teased by the wind-blown wave of your hair,
intoxicated by your sweat, rising,
steaming in the heat,
with its perfume of seduction
drugging me in transcendental suspension and vicious
        fantasy,
where you lay me bare
in an eternal nightly drama,
stripping me of my skin,
attaching my feathers
along the arched edges of your bow,
like an object of beauty
graced by your touch,
ignited by your tongue,
fire through your blood,
full as moon,

as water filling your thirsty bowl,
nourishing the green stem of your turquoise flower,
as I become moist and drunk,
made fresh from your nectar,

cooled in the shadow of your powerful brilliance.

Ocha

Crawling through the ground,
hidden and covered in slime,
begins the metamorphosis of the butterfly.

Almost at the point of death,
dormant, frozen in its prison,
asleep and unaware of its future,
until its casing presses tight,
breathless against its skin
as it stirs in its initiation,
pushing at the walls that hold
like a sealed coffin,
finding need for its own rebellion,
heaving its liberation song with calculated force,
a ritual guided,
pulled forward through a slight crack
like a beacon barely sighted over a stormy sea,
like the tender promise of a lover's kiss
after annihilation in the war of loneliness,
stretching out slowly,
limb after untrained limb,
emerging through its birth canal,
disoriented and dizzy,
unfolding one fan wing, then another,
to dry, visible and free over the fields,
revealing qualities of the prismatic universe

that powers it to flight,
to feast in the eternal garden,
empowered by itself
with beauty blazing mantle adorning its back,
head crowned luminous,
blessed by the eccentric wind,
blowing magnetically towards the midday sky,

receiving its final gift:
a left-sided wing,
invisible, perfumed,
trailing a direct spiral into heaven.

Nobody Knows My Name

I'm tired
dead anonymous tired
of getting mail addressed
to all those people I never was:

Gustazo	Peres
Gustavio	Penley
Gary	Porris
Gus	Perry
Gustaf	Pirey.

Nobody here knows my name.

This would never have happened in Havana.

Ghost Writing

I live with ghosts.
Laggard ghosts who wear their fatigue like a sheet
Petulant, unrepentant ghosts who never sleep
Ghosts like mouth sores
Ghosts that look me in the eye at midday
and buzz in my ears in the dead of night
Chinese laundry ghosts
Ghosts that tap and tease and taunt
Politically correct ghosts
Feminist ghosts
Holy ghosts
Ghosts of a chance

Gustavo-come-lately ghosts
Mami and *Papi* ghosts
The ghosts of all my Nochebuenas past.

My ghosts and I,
we have what you'd call this complicated relationship.
At this very moment, they tap tap tap tap tap
on the back of my head,
just behind my ears.
They know I'm listening, I pretend that I'm not.
But with every ghostly tap my spine vibrates
like a tuning fork.
If I could, I would leap to grab the greatest ghost
of them all and wring his neck like a wet towel.
But my life offers no such satisfactions.
The ghosts extract their pound of flesh
gram by gram, day by day.
You cannot sneeze them away.
They do not respond to treatment or medication
(my therapist is a ghost).

By now, the ghosts are more me than me.
One of them wrote this poem.

Bilingual Blues

Soy un ajiaco de contradicciones.
I have mixed feelings about everything.
Name your tema, I'll hedge,
name your cerca, I'll straddle it
like a Cubano.

I have mixed feelings about everything.
So un ajiaco de contradicciones.
Vexed, hexed, complexed,

hyphenated, oxygenated, illegally alienated,
psycho soy, cantando voy:
You say tomato,
I say tu madre;
You say potato,
I say Pototo.
Let's call the hole
un hueco, the thing
a cosa, and if the cosa goes into the hueco,
consider yourself en casa,
consider yourself part of the family.

Soy un ajiaco de contradicciones,
un pure de impurezas:
a little square from Rubik's Cuba
que nadie nunca acoplara.
(Cha-cha-cha.)

La Curandera

She shuffles to the door on faded scuffs.
Her breasts sway beneath the bodice of her muu-muu,
but the hands that welcome me are warm,
the skin like old paper crumpled then smoothed.
She is *la curandera*, faith healer. She is my *nana*.
We face each other, child to grandmother,
the trusting balance of young to old.
"*Mija*, did you give it to the priest, did he
bless it?" she asks. She takes the emblem
of the brown-skinned Virgin from my palm.
The sun is in her face, her eyes water.
Some say she can read minds. "It's for tonight,"
she says, "the *novena* for Don Jose."
She makes us drink a tea called *gordo lobo*,
fat wolf, when we are sick with fever from the flu.
She prescribes a tea of *estrella de anis*
to calm the itching rash of measles;
a tea of *manzanilla* for those who can't sleep.
The new Irish priest didn't understand.
"Witchcraft," he snorted, and refused to bless
the scapular. So at Mass I placed the badge
with its rubbed smooth image in my prayer book
hoping to catch stray blessings. *Kyrie eleison*.
Tonight the old women of the neighborhood
begin a *novena*, nine days of prayer
for a dying man. Doña Juanita attends,
her black lace shawl clipped to her bun.
Her husband lies on their bed at home swaddled
in sheets fresh from the line. The women fan
their black damask skirts on the red Windsor chairs.

Nana displays the scapular. Hail Mary's rise,
and I slip three steps from grace. I can
never go to heaven if the old man dies.

When Living Was a Labor Camp Called Montgomery

Back in the forties, you joined the family each summer to sort
dried figs. From Santa Maria to Gilroy, Brawley to Stockton,
you settled in rows of red cabins hidden behind the orchards.

You recall how the red cabin stain came off on your fingers,
a stain you pressed to your cheeks so you looked like
Dolores del Rio, the famous Mexican actress.

Her high-sculpted glow stunned the guys who dogged you
to the theater, the coolest building in town, where you escaped
the San Joaquin heat and fruit flies.

You wiggled in velvet-backed chairs, split popcorn with your
cousins. When the film's hero, the rancher's son, rode horseback
to the river and spied Dolores washing her hair, you'd swoon.

Just for a moment, a small eternity, the hero's hacienda, its dark
wood beams and low-slung chandelier, were yours. You were tall
and thin and everything looked good on you.

To tell the truth, though, you preferred Lauren Bacall's whistle.
So at the packing shed you eyed your brothers' friends, not
the pickers, the carpenters, those who wanted

out of the fields. You picked one with a full-mouthed smile, not
your mother's choice, but a tall man with papers who wanted
to join the army and live in L.A.

And perhaps, in the end, everything didn't look good on you:
maybe your hair didn't look good auburn; maybe
pillow-breasted women weren't meant to wear sheaths.

You visit the camp each summer reunion. Your sisters snatch
peeks at your husband. His teeth still look good. A cousin
glides you through a *cumbia*; you dreamt he kissed you once.

You catch the stench of rotting figs, of too-full outhouses. The
nose closes off. You feel how hot it was to sleep two to a
mattress, the only other room a kitchen.

You thought your arms thickened long ago lugging trays of figs.
You thought you had peasant ankles. You thought you could
     die in
the camp and no one would know your smell.

GUY GARCIA

Day of the Dead

In the keen obsidian night, lost
On a lightless street in a nameless town
We ask directions in splintered Spanish
as a white dog howls and seems to vanish.

Cameras, tapes and pens in hand, blindly
We've come to see to hear and know
What's in our blood but not our head
The dance of ghosts that's never dead.

Across a ditch and mounds of earth, seething
Between the graves and flowering trees
The crowd reflects its buried past
in a riot of masks and stamping feet.

At the molten core of the shouting throng, twirling
to the eternal tattoo of the fleeting song,
Witches, demons and holy ghouls
lean and lurch with laughing fools.

I ask the man beside me, reeling
what the mirrored masks are hiding
And feel the air outside my skin
tug at something deep within.

You want to understand? he says, smiling
And offers me a drink as a grinning devil
snags my eye, daring me to follow

I lift the cup of dreams and swallow.

Red Line

Under the calloused surface of the city, collar up, teeth
gritted, a blaring PA speaker defies me to understand it
as I watch my breath unfurl on the piss-perfumed platform
of the uptown-bound Interborough Rapid Transit

Before the seismic rumble, before the siren steel song
a light blooms in the black tonsils of the tunnel
first nothing, then so faintly coming on
an incandescent sunrise in the rat-infested dawn

The doors jerk open and we sit together, hip to hip,
shoulder to shoulder, stranger to sister, brother to other
Above my head a cardboard poster asks, "Pregnant?
        Addicted?
Infected? Get help fast."

I close my eyes against the warning signs
Glad you're waiting at the end of the line
confectionery contours swathed in creamy folds of down
to dream is only human, to doze divine

I wake from your arms at the jolt of Penn Station
bruised with the need for communion, ventilation
as buttoned-down pairs fend off leather clad stares
to the scratch of a Walkman, the listener unaware

A bum no longer vertical at Columbus Circle
his snores break like waves against New World shores
the flotsam of his spirit washed up at our feet
gets only fleeting glances as the subway advances

A woman staggers by with a cup in her hand
eyes hit the floor, a single coin drops
hurling together in a subterranean blur
the fare is collected, the ride never stops

Lourdes Gil

Outline for a Cuban Folk-Dance

For the quiet marlins at dusk
there's no desire harboring in the dark.
Yet you left hurriedly aroused
by premonitions
read in the erratic pattern of the rainfall.
The tides that never reached us
swallow the child absorbed in pressing twigs
on the pink sand
and set her free on the other side.
I thought of ribbons
distant shadows
streamers and red kites against the wind.

There's no desire left beneath the skin.
No marlins hushed in the fresh sunset.
No voices in the rain
washing through the spiraling wisteria.
Nothing that I can truly hear
or smell or possibly
mysteriously remember. I go about
polishing copper pots and silver
candlesticks. I rearrange the lies.
Travel from place to place.
Cool chickpea stew as I await.

When you return I hear the muffled fall
of acorns.
You retrieve the unplayed, open accordion
from the chair
and let it fall unharmed on your deliberate
search. You have indeed forgotten

the vase so delicately traced
with early tamarind
from your patio in Havana.

I now know
we sat too long between the acts.
Your shoulder brushes against the arc
of my name. It whispers old Assyrian riddles.
In rising tones recites in an Ionian dialect.
But the meanings are all lost
in the staleness of dead tongues.
Are these papyrus scrolls, I wonder,
beneath the reddened sponges of mamey
inside your brain?
Do you ever lament for the loss of the land
as you sway to the beat of a native dance-step?

Prague, 1924

You perhaps hear the song of the survivors
beneath the crescent moon
Marina Tsvetayeva
as you reconstruct the old city squares
and the silky cobwebs writhing
on medieval cobblestones
in the impossible landscape of your Russian signs.

Everything is about to ripen
as you shudder
in the obscure homelessness of Prague.
Or has your poem of the End
already taken shape inside your mind,
its languor like a liquid veil over
the bitter lines of an elliptical verse?

Everything is about to disembowel.
The gradient moon gleaming like an axe
pounding on syllables of discontent
suspended on rickets of denial.
The ghosts of pilgrim anchored in the ice
flinching high over your children's heads.

Everything is about to crumble around you.
A vision of death
glides over the moon like a spectacular mountain.
The mountain is a kingdom, you say.
But when the formidable giant collapses
you say: God is a growing baobab,
another god above him.

The river brightens, gurgles even
with its knowledge of rumors
and elegies of rumor. Can it bring back
in its wide-winding flow
the mirror that reflects your image into space
to rearrange the world to your design again?

MAGDALENA GÓMEZ

Mestiza Legacy

The ships have left the harbor,
    the ghosts remain.
Whips, leather long ago,
    crafted now in silence
and absent looks.

The ships have left the harbor,
    the ghosts remain.
The child looks to her mother for strength;
    Mother has no time.

            Mother is cleaning
            always cleaning,

            with water,
            with spit,
            with blood;

cleaning,
always cleaning.

            this is a ceremony
            which is no ceremony;

            it is meaning without healing,
            it is death without joy,
            it is life without sorrow,
            it is dance without spirit;

            it is only clean.

The ships have left the harbor,
     The ghosts remain.

The child looks to her father for love,
     he is hunting, always hunting;
               with hands
               with feet
               his body
               exposed

to the elements.

The hunter tangled in the net he never saw,
wounded by the bullet
he cannot find,
choked by the tears
that will not come
he hunts.

There is no time for love;
a liquid fire dance burns.

This is a dance
which is no dance.
               it is meaning without healing,
               it is death without joy,
               it is life without sorrow,
               it is dance without spirit;

it is only ceremony.

The ships have left the harbor,
     the ghosts remain.

The child looks to herself for healing,
finds meaning in
dances, ceremonies.

She finds no life,
she finds no death.

She must go to the harbor
where the ghosts remain.

Telling

it is 1992
500 years since Columbus
dug the heel of his boot
in the white Caribbean sand
leaving a stain that an eternity
of tides will not wash to sea

the blade of his sword
sharpened on the nails of the Cross
Columbus set sail
on the journey to another crucifixion
raising his eyes for the blessing
of the one he was about to condemn
having been made in the image of God
he feared no error
as long as the crucified
did not look like himself

tho bows of his ships
forced open the legs of the sea
as thcy forged towards paradise
in raging storms of greed

torching fear with the fire of avarice
Columbus of Genoa
beloved of Spain
shit over the rail
onto the face of God

yes, he did eat
and shit
and piss and fuck

see him standing over a hole
pulling down on the branches of trees
at his first encounter
with a platano

now see him laugh
at his first encounter
with people who had nothing to hide

now see him admire their ways
and see him covet the breasts and vaginas of their women
see him take a child
and peel her open
like a ripened fruit
see his mouth twist with envy at the ease with which they
        live
and how little they need to flower

see him covet tiny bits of gold
they carried as reminders of the sun

see him now
see him
sharpen his blade
on the nails of the cross
chopping native hands and ears
for daring to keep
what they did not have

see a people die without hands
the pools of their blood
turned as silt for the soil

remember the sting of the iron
as you pressed a shirt
a splatter from the boiling kettle
and let the memory touch
the soft part of your belly

imagine a gang of men at your front door
bearing a cross and a flag
they are seeing your neighborhood for the first time
they have just discovered it

they tie you to a chair
and gag you with a strip of your finest garment
digging their heels into your bed
they jump with delight
that they have found you

they take you to the toilet
where they soak your head
until you tell them where you keep your
wedding ring
and your baby's bronze shoes

they take your children
and tie them to a tree
on your perfect lawn
and soak them in gasoline

see your daughter for the last time
as ten men take her from behind
laughing as they come
one by one by one

they draw and quarter your dog
one limb at a time

they laugh in delight
that they have discovered
what they had not known before

and there will be no more children
with the hues of your eyes
and the traditions and stories of your family
will die unknown

there will be no more children

when you think of them
think of yourself
there will be no them
or us

when you think of Columbus
wrap the skin of a people
tainos
around your bones
and you will find another way
to tell the story of Columbus

It Happens While Presidents Play Golf

Norberto washed up on a Florida shore
in 1952
and drove his passion
straight to Tampa
where he jumped out
at the first red light
to have a sandwich
at the whites only restaurant
he got as far as the table
when he took off his hat

he was duly informed
that the nigger chow hole
was across the street
there he was told
it was a colored place
he should leave without
making a scene thank you

Norberto bought a sandwich
in a shack behind a gas pump
and found a doorway
where he could eat in peace
with los bones
who were too dazed
to begin to figure out
what color he was
or to care
alcoholism has certain advantages
in a world where reason
takes the place of being human

Norberto told los bones
about Fidel
and how he has to admire his cojones
and the way he blows his smoke
in the face of opposition
and how you can hate a man's guts
and still see his worth

Los bones rolled Buglers
and with great respect
for this mayor of the doorway
chucked raspy ah ha's
from the far end of their caves

Norberto tossed his hat
on the pyre
where another day

would rest in peace
and los bones
would warm their hands

Norberto set sail
on the heels of his slippers
leaving his brothers
with the blessing of Yemaya

feeling the coins in his pocket
he promised Chango a cigar
in thanks
and moved in certainty
along the waves
of good-bye

RAY GONZALEZ

The Recurring Dream of the Snakes
as a Gift for My Aching Shoulder

1

I saw a rattlesnake eaten by another rattler.

2

I saw an egg break open to reveal
the yoke of eternity is the liquid
pouring heat on my injured shoulder,
a snake coiling its muscle into my muscle,
my shoulder blade a shield
against the striking head.

3

I saw the snake coil as if this circle
empowered it to take me away
from what gave me life,
the den in volcanic rock beckoning
my closed eyes to drop into
the smoke of eggs.

4

I saw one snake belong in the tree
and one snake fill the flower

73

to form a pollen that spread
for thousands of years,
a trust in what comes out
of the earth to make me pass
through the occasion of sleep.

5

I saw a snake swim into the hole
where I built a fort of sand,
its low walls protecting me
from the hidden white lake
about to rise, explode,
and shower me with venom.

6

I saw a snake devour a shoe.
I wanted it to contain my foot.

7

I saw the rattle erect
inside the skull of salt.
I saw it rattle,
then I heard the beat
enter my stomach,
pass through me as the drum
I tore when I started believing.

8

I saw the body meet the soul
as it shed its skin,

left it clinging on a low branch,
a slight breeze rustling it
as I touched the brittle designs,
thought of the thief growing weary
with nothing to steal.

9

I saw the fang lift in the other self,
disappear in the cake of flesh,
recalled how I first recognized a snake
by entering the canyon upon birth,
trying to open my eyes without wisdom
of the slithering umbilical,
the harsh rope of holding onto
the seed that shaped the fang.

10

My shoulder hurts as I watch
the snake lie still,
accept my recurring cycle,
remove it from my shoulder
like the extended arm
of mournful poison that put me to sleep.

How?

*We were told that bodies rising to heaven lose their vulvas,
their ovaries, wombs, that her body in resurrection becomes
a male body.*

—Susan Griffin

She died, did not become as male,
but a memory in the garden,
a flower of thought following me,
thinking I knew something about women
when all I had was the father
who never spoke to me because his mother died
and went to heaven when he was five,
her vulva cutting his tongue,
casting it into a cloud of ovaries
hovering over the quiet sons.

She died and he became
a man of the street, knowing
he could never speak to his son
because the resurrection says
you will be punished for
losing the mother so young,
rising to heaven without
telling him her story.

She died and never cut
the umbilical cord until
she crashed into the hidden life,
the fist her son carried
in his groin as he grew up,
fathered a son, dreamed
of other bodies leaving
because they obeyed him

as he got away with what he did,
turning his back on the family

waiting to be fertilized toward heaven,
the boy and girls confusing sex
with the natural shame of the earth
where living and dead mothers
tell them not to look up,
or gaze at the water that opens
the wombs of a long life
of silent answers and mute sons.

Homage to Lucian Blaga

1. Brief Beginning

*Be glad on the blossom and understand we don't have
to know now who brings and spreads fire.*

—Lucian Blaga, early twentieth-century Romanian poet

We know the flame kisses
what we believed in.

We take the mystery of invasion
against the great burning,

find a way to guess what
presence breathes fire,

which companion
shares water.

We hold the match to the finger,
paint a change of skin upon ourselves

as punishment for not knowing
when to strike,

not accepting this branding is the way
of learning the language of smoke.

2. Heaven and Earth

Astir under the trees God makes himself smaller to give the red mushrooms room to grow under his bark.

—Lucian Blaga

He lies down to fill
the earth with poison.
He is under the leaves
exciting the ground to stand erect,
red mushrooms pushing through
to spit at the world
like the tiny demons escaping
the embrace of a god
they never thought would come down.

3. Fate

In sleep my blood draws me back into my parents like a wave.

—Lucian Blaga

Entering their bodies,
I see why it happened this way,
recall the first words ever cried,
seconds after birth,
their sound an incoherent message
for them to let go,
let me come out and wait for the answer,
so I could grow the way
I should have gone,
make it through this passage
without having to look back
at their hesitation, postponement,
desire, consummation,
without having to take the wrong turn
into the belly of their soul.

4. Asking

> *Look, the stars are coming into the world at the*
> *same time as my sorrowful questions.*
>
> —Lucian Blaga

How far do they travel before
we wish they would explode?
When was the last time we spoke
the same instant a falling star
streaked over our heads?
How much do I have to reveal
without using their light?

Who decides stars have something more
than their burning energy?
Why do we continue to overlook the comet?
Where do they go after we see?

How can we trust the universe
when it expands without us?
Why do we insist on looking up?
What does sorrow have to do
with that oncoming mass of light?

5. Without Regret

> *How humbly bends the arrogant forehead of*
> *yesterday's ecstasy.*
>
> —Lucian Blaga

Last night, we gave it everything,
clutched each other,
couldn't catch our breaths,
or follow each other
to the peak of our breasts.
We kept at it all night,
hurried through love to reach
the morning as one body,
gave up identity before ecstasy,

allowed the naked body to find out,
a flesh-driven need to escape from desire
so we could face the world demanding
we fall before a creator,
a still, moist ground that insists
on punishing the lovers who rolled
out of its vast reach.

6. Back

> I stand turned toward my country—return is a
> dream I can't wake from.
> —Lucian Blaga

I am constantly returning,
going back across the border
where the river rose and fell,
dried before me like a dream
of crossing a great canyon
opening toward the frontier,

my nameless country where I settle
as the man who got this far
by turning his back
on mountains of a lost child.

I can't wake from this dream
of coming back to see
if the desert rains cracked everything,
revisit old adobe where I found answers
cut into the walls like a map carved
by those preceding me into the dream,

the point where I fell
into the deep water
upon finding myself at home,
about to wake up.

Memory of the Hand

The hand recalls what it has held,
the fist of truth wedged inside the knuckles,

fitting into the drum of things you cared about,
lifting its memory to allow you

to be alone when
you are not alone,

forcing you to reach out, take care
of that memory you made up with your hands,

the one about taking your father's arm
you have never held,

helping him cross the street
where you let him go

without waving goodbye or making
a fist at him in anger.

The band aches for what it has held,
mist washing its fingers like smoke

where you hid your knowledge
of a sign language, a movement of joints,

palms and fingers trying to spell
that silent moment when

you touched what moved out
of your reach—

a soft yearning, a bare back,
the tiny mountain range of spine rising

to remind you the hand holds onto little flesh,
knows nothing about the skin except lines

on its own palms, deep furrows where
the weight of remembrance is held.

César A. González-T.

B.C.: Before Clinton

4
8 years
I slipper-clumped down
this split level
        [after wresting with the night,
            somehow forged a way into today]
to my automatic whirred garage
door down
there to my
a.m.'d paper,
        [thumped headlong, folded and warm
            the rite way]
opened,
        [loosed and tugged the string]
seen the same tight manufactured grin
 and daily, . . . like prayers
 I said: "Simple-minded ass!
                    Pinche Creature!"
        [They buy it! They buy it!
        Oh my great Jesus
        Christ
        They buy it!]

Eight years of rage later
we Americans
had a few too many
votes
and got that way again.
Then we elected to be led
by a CIA professional terrorist,
believing we are God's divinely destined

83

amongst us,
incarnating freedom,
even if we have to rape the world
to send a little business our way

Now we'll see
if it's O.K.
4
ever.

"Damn!"

Sometimes he'd be washing the car
... all by himself
and he'd say, "Damn!"
or sweeping the last dry morsels of leaves
onto an old dustpan
saved just for outside
for when he was alone
in the silence of a summer afternoon
he'd say, "Damn!"
He didn't go to his abuelita's funeral
He wasn't there when his father died
He was with someone else he loved,
and he wasn't there the moment she died
Y le pesaba, sabes?
An anvil of loneliness
would fall into his chest
and he'd say, "Damn!"

Rain Lantern

My words are fried plantains
Your face is full of landslides
Whenever tonight sits down
on the hot tin roof of experience

Quetzalcoatl arms the blows
of slow lingering tomorrow
that grasp the edge of the street
with the brittle talons of darkness

Blood horizons and tourists don't mix
the sliding doors and clogged drains
only serve to collect the methane gas
where the repeating windows face
the smoking iguana of earthquakes

Walk the guava paste road
to the drowning clock of our anatomy
Your move begins to swell
as I set my jaw to meet the embers
of a falling balcony.

Tropical Weather Report

Cat fluids on the street
Cracks dividing the color of moth wings
Dead dry season of cactus plain south
where only a hummingbird expands the stains
of flowers sleeping under a lizard's dream

as skin absorbs the black centipede
Eyes multiply the ammunition
of floods and other seductions
feeding rivers with disasters
cutting the underground cables
Storms are announced from ground zero
to the murky waters of basements
Desire the multitude of rain
dancing the poetry of paso fino horses
of mango flight
and moist sleep under a tin roof
whatever is stationary is forecast hot
whatever blows is wild
All bets are off

The Structure of a Dream

A butterfly is a buddhist tomb
underneath the vapor of a lizard's breath
It dashes the dust of a thousand suns
among the broken hands of rusting clock
The sweep of its wings
embraces the African coast
where the equator is the last anthill
before the burning ocean
and the wind is a door
that opens the wounds
of ten thousand ruins upon the plain
of a manati's eye
Flowing through the mambo slits
that appear again and again
in the coffee cups
of aging windows

JUAN FELIPE HERRERA

Southern California Nocturne (Circa 1964)

for Tommy Landale

He used to come pick me up in a baby blue TR-3 Triumph
and we'd spin out to the East side of the city and shoot a
funny 30-30 that some Chicano crazy on German marches
gave you. So we'd hit it—splitting rocks the size of an
elephant's ear. Man, your room, Tommy, believe me, it was
like a sail boat gliding over Mission Hills into my dreams.
I'd be cruising. And then we'd box in your garage. Your mom
looking out the window to make sure you didn't crack my
skull. How about those 250 sit-ups on a slant, Jack! The
dude was beautiful. Blue-green eyes, short blond curly hair.
Rosy cheeks, French style. Sometimes, I would go downstairs
to your kitchen and check out the goods in store. Anise seed.
Basil. Marjoram—what the hell is that? Asshole. Thyme (is
this what Simon and Garfunkel were singing about? Come
on!), mustard powder. That's it for me! Your mom strolls in
carrying a long gift box and breaks open a silver and black
dress she just bought at the Broadway. I am looking at
Tommy's mom. She's a lawyer. Young. She's thinking of
sponsoring Beto Urista, my best friend, so he can go to Chap-
man College. She's pretty. I bet you she can dance the Twist,
easy. Her hair style is off, just a bit; kind of a Clark Kent
fondue. It's dinner time. I swear, this is weird. Your dad has
those tanned sinewy Popeye arms that are common to MD's.
I don't know why, but it's true. His white pressed shirt
sleeves are carefully rolled up. Your younger snot-nosed sister
sits quietly and Jeanne, the oldest, is probably hanging out
with Hugo tonight. Hugo Repetto is Beto's cousin from
Mexico City. He's always talking about Sartre, Jobim and
Pasternak. And Beto, who's the same age can't get off of
Nietzsche, Freud and Thelonious Monk! I wonder what it'll

be like when Tommy and me get into 10th grade? The food here looks like the kind Jules Verne—in *20,000 Leagues Under The Sea*—would eat: billowy white shit splashed on giant hamburger urchins. But, I am cool. And Tommy is wolfing it. Tommy wants to be a writer. What on earth is he talking about? He used to come pick me up in a baby blue TR-3 Triumph and we'd fly. 100 mph is slow, ok? Right! You made my nose bleed motherfucker! Boxing, shit! The dude was at least six feet tall! You had everything Tommy! And you still came over, all across town, down 16th and up "F" Street by the Sunbeam Bakery right next to the Thrifty Bread store front knock on my door—Is John home? And it was me and my mom who was still getting dizzy spells, always aching and my books like the *World As Will and Idea* that blew the social worker's mind one day when she came to do the usual goddamn Welfare evaluation and to peep and see if we were living with someone and therefore committing Welfare fraud so she asked me innocently like she would all the other boys South of Broadway Street what are you doing? And I said reading Schopenhauer you fucking bitch because that's my bag along with Zen and John Coltrane in that green house with a thousand apartments and a thousand hunchback shadows on a hill overlooking the freeway South to Tijuana and North to Whoknowswhere. What's a writer? Why do you want to be a writer? I should have asked you. Let's go to Mission Beach and body surf. Yeah! I heard you were locked up in some detention center or boarding school in Arizona. Arizona! What you doing? Frying potatoes for the nation? Just kidding asshole. Not too long ago, I ran into your younger sister on the stairs to the mezzanine at the University of Washington in Seattle. What's snot-nose's name, anyway? She told me, Tommy is dead. Suicide? She didn't want to give me any details. But, I remember. Just you. Your breezy dare-devil eyes, big wide bronze Mission Beach shoulders. Shooting guns in the back country, by Ramona, at fifteen. Your house, my house. Your mom, my mom. Your jazzy race across the asphalt. You and me. Where were we going Tommy? From where, what point?

To write what? To dance around an ash-colored canvas, laughing out loud like dogs as we punch each other's arms? To a pastel blue torn tin of memories? What do you remember, Tommy?

The Sea During Springtime

Come down to this stony day
—an evening when I lift my head.

Gaze at the architecture,
greenish and sealed.

Peasant shadows and hours pouring from the skin.
It isn't a burial mound I am looking at.

It is lost beneath the lead and wood
and the angles of my pressing mouth.

I cannot drink from its tides.
It is a sea that will open in another sky.

There is only a white tiger
pacing beneath the black.

Designs inside my bones.
Aurelia Quintana is dead.

Laundry faith woman, solitary soup overseer
in an oven for holy brooms.

I circle her from a distance
in *el Valle de San Joaquin.*

My uncle lifts her from a candle-like bench
shaped by silence and his captive soul.

My aunt smells of plants tonight—lavish,
thick-lipped, wet and spinning in the jade center.

There are more shadows, embossed,
carved with my solemn left hand.

The burnisher that I keep is well defined and alive.
I earn this knife from dirt and apartment lamps.

I earn the kerosene and accordion smoke.
Once my mother hid there while she was kissing.

Once I wept there and saw my father leave.
He was leaving the same way we left every city.

Now my spirit pushes me towards the tower.
No one is there—except my grandfather, Alejo.

He is the man who cut *maguey*,
pulled whitish juice from a pointed heart.

He is the worker who turned to salt. *Pulque*
down the arms. A tiny soul slobbering birth.

I am carrying the dead. I can hear them
nibble my ears with their faint tongues.

Late hours—a spirit sits on my head.
Then it throws my legs to one side.

I raise my hand and grab at night air,
silvery in its grain.

Silvery in its oceans. Silvery
in its feminine voices.

You never visited.
You walked the streams.

When you told me, singing,
I saw your dead child.

He was locked away, beneath
Briars and merciless woods.

After he fell,
No one looked for him.

And now!
And now!

The waters are yellow and blue by the trail,
reflecting the oval sky.

A boat rushes with women, men and children.
Dark hair and swaying torsos.

An old man with a reddish beard stands
alone by the sails, laughing.

He asks me to cross this bluish bridge
where people lean over and gaze.

A water color of green and shredded violet
comes to light my face again.

There are gulls in the air. A black hat.
Carnations, crescent disks. Prayer.

A little battle for heat. Naked
without a jacket, grayish. I give thanks.

My belly is deep into the sod. A baby boy
in cottons and pomegranate flush calls me too.

Three steps above me. Two roses above his head,
bowed. He is a wheel of concentric infinities.

I can place my tears on his round arms.
I can place my death on his shoulders.

Above the ground, in my stupor
—this is the way I walk.

A black pagoda comes up through the waves.
I am full of beginnings. I am full of wonderings.

String music. Mussels and sea bark.
Clams as flint and pursed as castanets.

An open palm inside. Aurelia leans
by the grasses. Her legs cross the sands.

Aurelia pulls her rings and shawls,
soft and earthen. We dance in a full circle.

Around the coral. She steps into a wider ring.
Water washes my feet, goes up into my navel.

Another wave thrashes the satin arm of my spirit.
I am ready to sing. My aunt Lela weeps.

Aurelia sits on a parchment—
the one my mother carried since she was a girl.

It is made of fibers and leaves gathered on the way.
She is young. She is restless and slides down a rock.

Her hair long—going. Snow and sunlight
in the winds. It is springtime.

It must be springtime in the mountains
where the sea begins.

Sorting Miami

I pale my cheek against the pane
as the runway jolt blurs us into our city.
—Ricardo Pau-Llosa

I watch them unnoticed
from the cement railing outside
the Jose Marti YMCA, its glass doors locked for the day.

Tomatoes, limes, onions
hang in cellophane bags
from the rusted van.

Crates of papayas and avocados
surround this old vendor still smiling
after 11 years on the same street corner.

Friends take turn in the shade
exchanging stories
from a distant canvas.

A middle aged woman, fighting a lost battle,
protects herself
with her red umbrella.

A young woman struggles
to push the baby carriage
along the brick sidewalk.

A Bronco pulls up
to buy its share
of the tropics.

I understand their voices,
and the silhouette of the vendor
could easily be that of my uncle, now dead in Havana.

But in minutes,
I drive across a deep fissure
in the asphalt.

I wonder how long will I be able
to step into this mirror of a city
and return home in one piece.

Finding Home

I have travelled north again,
to these gray skies
and empty doorways.
Fall, and I recognize
the rusted leaves descending
near the silence of your home.
You, a part of this strange
American landscape with its
cold dry winds,
the honks of geese and
the hardwood floors. It's more
familiar now than
the fluorescent rainbow on the overpass,
or the clatter of politicos in the corners,
or the palm fronds falling by the highway,
I must travel again, soon.

An Unexpected Conversion

Mother hid from us the blue and white beads
her nanny, Brigida,
had given her, and the plate of
pennies in honey under the Virgin's skirt.
She rarely spoke about the island,
never taught us to cook black beans.

Father played Stravinsky and Debussy on Sundays.
Once, he relented and taught us the guaguanco.
He swore, as she did, they would never go back.
He's thirty years in exile and
about to retire.

But today, mother and I sit in the garden.
She rests on the edge of an old rusted swing
and speaks of reconstruction,
of roads and houses; "I know they'll
need an experienced engineer," she says looking at dad.
Her hair blows gently in the breeze.

I've never seen her look so young.
I've never felt so old.

El Elvis

El Elvis
    puro pedo
        bien chingón

On a traffic light island
    on the corner of
        pobresa and maltrato

Hollering
    "NARANJAS BIEN DULCES!"
    at the insulated conquistadores del
        oro y plata

Con sus patillas largas
Como latigo quemanto
Como pólbora en el aire bailando

El Elvis
    with his upper lip twitching
    but fingers too thick
    to play with guitar strings

Voice too rough to carry
    the high notes

Rust skin
    too dry & unpleasant
    for the mannequin dolls
    of pale soul rolling by

El Elvis
    de Mezcal Dreams
    & beer can nightmares
    De piramide ancestors
    & high-rise offsprings

"NARANJAS BIEN BIEN DULCE CABRONES!
Cinco pesos la bolsa. Aqui estoy
y no me voy."

Family

It's all about grandmothers
with big floppy ears,
and coughing grandfathers,
with jello stomachs laughing.

It's all about five t.v. sets
full blast on different channels.
Manic,
Phlegm spitting,
Toupee wearing,
Real Estate crazed uncles.

It's all about friends on Xanax,
rotting amputated thumbs,
friends on coke
on the open heart surgery slab.

It's all about drunken bouts
in station wagons on quiet
Baton Rouge lawns,
speeding.
Late night vulture calls,
behind fifteen year old bushes
and atop carved tree branches.

It's all about
caffeine midnights at Norms,
liquor vomit on parking lots,
and youth spent effortlessly.

The Spy

His ex-wife,
twenty years younger
decided burning his body
would be the least expensive
alternative.
He lived next door
and was a likable
character
in his early
sixties.
Overcoat and wide-rim
hat were his trademark,
and his gray sprinkled
mustache
hid the everpresent polite smile.
I was told
he had left Cuba
in the late 50s,
and worked as a
waiter for a few
years in Paris,
France, before coming to America.
He never said much,
but his eyes I'll
never forget.
His eyes,
when I was certain he
had at one point

been the spy
who had saved the world,
and his eyes,
when overnight
his mind was lost
and he was placed in the old folks home
by the railroad tracks.

Juana La Loca

I

Juana
who was mad
carried Felipe's body
in its coffin
for years.

You
who are not mad,
how will you carry
my memory
when I leave you?

II

She knew
without Felipe
the water would turn black,
the air foul,
and the crops would die
in the fields.

Who
would have believed her?
It happened
five hundred years ago.
Everyone thought
she was crazy then.

Christmas at the Health Care Center
on the West Mesa

My aunt is a wisp of curled hair,
Tiny cumulonimbus clouds circling
Her ninety years of life.

Outside, the contrails of great jets
Streak through the clear blue sky.
There is seldom snow in the singular

Motions of the winter of New Mexico.
Ah, but when the snow falls
It brings out the child to play!

We move toward some Christmas rendezvous
Each our own way as best we can
Across the nursing home landscape.

Her world bound by the frontier
Of wheelchair to bed
And bed to wheelchair, my aunt

Dances round and round inside her head.
She dances back to the thirties and twenties
And says she loves me very much.

I give her a toy to pass the time.
It changes color to the touch.
Now she makes her own rainbows

As she talks of the small angels
Who sang all morning in choir
Moving from room to room.

My aunt chatters on and on.
She is dancing to some faraway desire
Caught up in her own deep song.

She is dancing toward the bright light.
She is dancing toward Bethlehem
Deep in the interior of the nursing home.

We hear off in the distance a ghost train
Whistling to a crescendo
Then fade, Doppler effect, into a moan.

I think of Van Gogh's whirling stars
Turning the dark to a blinding white,
Fred Astaire and his dazzling smile,

And for me there is no regret.
I hear great-grandfather's violin
Cracked and silenced a long time ago.

It plays the tunes he must have played
At weddings, funerals, gatherings like this.
Those songs are like the missing voices

From the old photograph in the album
All this is about to become.

Discourse of the Severed Head
of Joaquin Murieta

—*excerpt from the play,* The Ballad of
Joaquin Murieta, *first performed by La
Compania del Teatro de Albuquerque.*

From the waters of my mother's womb
I fell head first into the world.
I walked the land and came to know
The great beasts of the earth,

Also the lizard scurrying across sandstone,
The eagle and the hawk in the sky
And the ever-watchful buzzard.

Thieves and murderers
Severed my head, tore it
Like a ripe fruit
From a tree in full bloom
And dropped it here in this cold glass jar.

My head swirls in this filthy tomb.
I see the bleary-eyed drunkards at dawn.
I weep unseen tears in these waters
When I see myself through the eyes of drunkards.
I reach out with their leaden arms.
I stumble about on their uncertain legs.

Before I was twenty, I was as good as a Comanche
With a horse. My head thrown back,
My jaw open, I sucked in the wind.
Until my lungs took on a wild ecstasy.
Now only dark waters flow into my mouth
And out again to this cloudy and closed sea.

With Carmelita I came to California
To work the mines of the land.
Here I found men more beasts than men.
Their blows drove me to the deep canyon
Where all the rivers gathered and waited for me.
Now only dark waters flow into my mouth
And out again to this glass-bound sea.

My head turns and turns in this filthy jar.
I see the bleary-eyed drunkards at dawn.
Once my eyes caught the sun's fire
Burning through pine on a mountain ridge.
When Carmelita laughed, leaves shimmered

And even the doe paused in joy with her fawn.
Birds flew with a fluttering of wings.

Driven to the deep canyon, I became
The outlaw they wanted me to be.
Raiding through the California night,
With red-rimmed eyes I aimed and shot
My victims, the grim haters of life.

They forced me from the fields and the mines,
Violated Carmelita, then took my severed head
And let it fall like some broken bird
Into this miserable jar where it circles
Around and around in a dark and moldy sea.

DEMETRIA MARTÍNEZ

Hit and Run

Had you raped me my hate
would be radiant, sure of itself,
a memory in bruises
I could despise.
Instead we loved and sighed
from one new moon to the next...
then you left.

If I am pregnant I will abort,
expel you as readily as you did me,
plastic-lined can of limbs
and crushed skulls,
I, the doped-up murderess, exiting
the clinic, my insides bleached
clean, clean, what a coup,
even the gateway car awaits me.

Or, if I am pregnant, heavy with you,
a mountain, a cow, indifferent to all
but the clouds and this love
doubling inside me,
is it a girl? A head, pink and bruised,
bobs up between my thighs,
your lips and eyes,
but see how she loves me,
I am the victor here, leaving
the clinic with a pink bundle
of your best features,
your violence washed down the sinkhole
with the placenta.

Saintly, abstract:
loving you in her,
touch us and I'll
sink a knife into you, sir.

Discovering America

Santo Niño
on bedroom desk,
holy water in a
mouthwash bottle
grandma had
the priest bless,
my house was a
medieval city
you visited
but what you sought
was not here.

Not in wrists
oiled with sage,
Chimayó earth
sprinkled on sheets,
nor San Felipe bells
that pecked away
the dark,
Cordova blanket
we hatched
awake in.

To prove love
I shed still
more centuries,
rung by rung
down a pueblo kiva

you touched
the *sipapu,*
canal the universe
emerged from,
brown baby
glazed in
birthmuds.

You thought
America
was on a map,
couldn't see it
in a woman,
olive skin,
silver loops
in lobes,
one for each
millennium endured
on this husk
of red earth,
this *nuevo mejico.*

Last night
I dreamed
a map of the
continent,
the train
that took you
from me whipped
across tracks
like a needle
on a seam
somewhere
near Canada.

It took me
four years
to heal.

Have you?
Have you
discovered
America
or at least
admitted
a woman grew
maiz here
long before
you named it
corn!

DIONISIO D. MARTÍNEZ

Standard Time: Novena for My Father

We're turning back the clocks tonight
to live an hour longer.
I suppose this is a useless ritual to you now.

Late October brings life to the wind chimes
with that perpetually nocturnal music
so reminiscent of you.

I memorize a small song, a seasonable dirge
for the night that lives outside my
window. I call each note by name:
All Hallows Eve; All Saints Day; all the souls
in my music pacing, talking to themselves.

All day I sit by a statue of Saint
Francis of Assisi, birds on his shoulders,
nothing but faith in his hands.

At dusk I return to the house you knew
and a life you would probably understand.
There are night birds waiting to
breathe music back into the wind chimes when
the forecast calls for stillness.

I still remember what you said about belief,
how you laughed when I said I thought
the world could carry the cross I'd carved
around my shoulder and through my fist.

I let out one sigh that is almost musical.
I know you can hear this much.

I take a small step back and picture
you here before I light the last candle.

All the souls in hell couldn't set this world
on fire. Even if they prove that our lives
are mathematically impossible, we
will cling to the last flame in the equation.

Variations on Omar Sharif

All my uncles on my mother's side have looked
like Omar Sharif at one time or another.
The eyes, the forehead, the mustache.
Especially my uncle with the radio dream.
One afternoon he took all the silence
in the world and caught the bus to the amateur
show in Havana. My great-grandmother
heard his name on the radio and caught
the next bus.

My uncle had greased his hair for the occasion.
Years would pass before they'd hear the name
Omar Sharif, before they'd read it and see
his photograph in the tabloid my mother opened
daily, religiously, to the Hollywood page.
Hollywood had become a perfectly
acceptable religion by then.
Now it was just my uncle and my great-grandmother
and the radio. They called his name.
He held the microphone as if everything
depended on it. He held
his breath for a moment. Then he heard
the music and looked out at the small audience.
He saw his grandmother. The microphone

slipped from his hands. He took one slow
step backward. Then another step.

On the bus home he held the silence
like a consolation prize between his teeth.
He didn't know what to make
of his grandmother—her own silence,
her composed face. So he imagined his voice
on the radio and his grandmother crying.
He swallowed all the silence.

For a moment he could taste his own voice.

Victor Martínez

Unlucky Cracks

My legs hurt to go off and make decisions,
bring my stomach a full plate,
or simply join the great embrace of music and particle.
Arm in arm
with my brother the concrete
I walk toward the straw-fire hiss of the sun.

One foot sounds like it wants to believe, the other
is convinced of what it has learned to avoid:
unlucky cracks.

Cracks with wind travels through, pressing in its stomach,
cracks where space kissed cavities in the air,
cracks that with a dash sum up arrogantly in the center
our birth and death

I don't know why...
I don't know why
when I turn my eyes back inside my head, searching,
I find nothing
but the dry void of echoing cracks,
and beyond them, the beast
that slowly eats, morsel by morsel,
every last brick of my fortune.

The Sierras

I came down the slate hills of the sierras, past tin barns
scabbing with rust and tractors stiffening
after their last bite.

Crowds unraveled against the onrush of traffic,
sparrows nibbled the clouds gray from tree
to tree, and in a puddle of rain, breaths of wind made
jellies of buildings and lampposts.

Autumn, sucking back what was never given,
and the city, that great tumor among
greater tumors, was sweating through its pores
all the small miseries and joys from the same salt.

In a room, slanting on its shadows, overgrown with a quiet
seeping like dust from the ceiling, a woman I knew,
numb in the aloneness of her vision, fluttered her fingers
      along her dress—
a word unsaid, budding in the hollow of her mouth.

The Chase

They say the chase ends where the earth is put together
by two halves, but no matter—because that is you
at thirty, perhaps forty:
corpus callosum of the brain,
two loaves opening and closing like a book.

Your arms spring out and lungs push and pull
rinsing the midnight air—
but no matter, because you are there, chasing
the child of wonder and hope
through cities coffined in smog.

You missile through firs, through mouths dusted
with mathematical chalk.
You follow the muddy-water spillways peppered with
bacterial spore.

Not the shadow that greets itself in the dark
but the utter collision of evaporating rain
        leads you on.
Not the lightning's sketch but the black puzzle of night,
as you appear and disappear among people,
chasing he who knows your name
but won't tell.

JULIO MARZÁN

Ethnic Poetry

The ethnic poet said: "The earth is maybe
a huge maraca/ and the sun a trombone/
and life/ is to move your ass/ to slow beats."
The ethnic audience roasted a suckling pig.

The ethnic poet said: "Oh thank Goddy, Goddy/
I be me, my toenails curled downward/
deep, deep, deep into Mama earth."
The ethnic audience shook strands of sea shells.

The ethnic poet said: "The sun was created black/
so we should imagine light/ and also dream/
a walrus emerging from the broken ice."
The ethnic audience beat on sealskin drums.

The ethnic poet said: "Reproductive organs/
Eagles nesting California redwoods/
Shut up and listen to my ancestors."
The ethnic audience ate fried bread and honey.

The ethnic poet said: "Something there is that
doesn't love a wall/ That sends
the frozen-ground-swell under it."
The ethnic audience deeply understood humanity.

Ode

Long had we roamed the Upper East Side,
browsing galleries, windows, shops,

scaling the peaks of exquisite art
crafted to find its human counterpart:
Chinese armies on checkerboard onyx,
geometric designs by primitive psyches,
Pointillist trees, Impressionist traffic,
Cubist mammals of chrome bumper parts,
black and white slices of time's frozen river
uniquely cropped in camera shots. But

artifice paled before a huge white conch
like none tripped over on public beaches,
the same miraculous genital half shell
on which Venus was born a grown woman;
great art once free as the 6 P.M. sun's
bloody descent in a Sophoclean finish,
forty-five bucks in a rose-tinted cube.
Hand squeezing hand, we walk out, but my ear,
as if flat against glass hears a roar:
Beauty is money, money beauty. That's all
You know on earth, all you've ever known.

The Old Man

After the Crash,
no God spoke but money,
money the highest art
decorated his world,
now dented and tarnished,

whose brass surface
only murkily reflects
second-deck cabins,
muffled trumpet solos
as faded tuxedos lead
dully sequined gowns,

crossing the Atlantic
in lost younger lives,
heralds of an old deity
as unreliable as TV,
library novels,
even the latest news of ancient deceits,
so he tunes out
to shuffle from room
to identical room
in remolded slippers,

amenable to death's
preliminary offers
because the bald world's
tired somersaults
he knows by heart.

Calle de la Amargura

*In Havana there is a street called Calle
de la Amargura or Street of Bitterness.*

On the Street of Bitterness
a man runs from the rain
arms raised into the next imagination.

A woman sits head down
on the stoop of a house
where her indiscretions
fly about like butterflies.

All songs end,
memories soar over rooftops,
an eyelid swells with desire.

On the Street of Bitterness,
Calle de la Amargura, there are boys
scratching their tongues,
they dare not speak, they wait
their turn in the line of understanding.

On that street
a daughter is dying.
Her father searches for a cure
and finds instead the pillar of his wife,
covered with lizard scales,
melting with the rain.

On the Street of Bitterness,
Calle de la Amargura, no one is surprised
at the awful taste of Paradise.

Philadelphia

The coffee has redeemed itself by now.
I am awake enough to see you walking
down the street to your apartment
exhausted like a sparrow
after long work in the tenements.

You linger in my memory hunched a little,
tragic, hurt by men. The afternoon haze
is *cafe con leche* in the city,
the block busy with unemployed
latinos, sipping beer, playing
dominos, whispering deals at the corner.

Across the street the huge Lithuanian
church has become ridiculous.
Hardly anyone enters. Rhythm and form
fly away with the pigeons
and the river is a slab of dirty wood.
You turn the corner, disappear.
Philadelphia is awash in loss.
This is the dream the coffee drowned.

Cuba

> *... brillando contra el sol y contra los poetas ...*
> —Heberto Padilla

There it is, the long prow
of the Caribbean, charging to break
the map's complexion.
It is a key, a crocodile, a hook,
an uncoiling question,
a stretch of sinews catching
dribbles from the continent
under which it will, forever, float.

120

The island mouth is smiling
or frowning, who can tell,
stuffed with waning intentions,
sugarcane and sand.

Such a little place,
such an island listing against sorrow
in the middle of the ocean's gut,
playing make believe
queen of brine, dressing up in green
and calling forth its poets for praise,
its leaders for chesty boasts,
inventing for itself a pantheon
of tropical saints, a vast
and profound literature,
an epic history to rival Rome's.

There it is, pretending it shimmers
over the heads of its people,
denying the terror it feels
when no one listens, denying
that it is always almost drowning,
that it cannot help anyone, least
of all itself, that it is only
a strip of dirt between morning and night,
between what will be and what was,
between the birth of hope
and the death of desire.

EcologicHumanitarianIsm

There would be nothing wrong
                            with
        feeding the Wild Birds
                            of
                    the Forests,
                                keeping them
                        from hunger
                                    in
                                the dead of Winter
                                            ,If

    there were No Children
                        starving
        to their deaths
                    in the Spring
                        of their Lives
                            in this World.

If Every Human Need Were Fed,
                            If every Dream
                                    fulFilled
                                        What a Thrill!
        it would be then
                    to feed Pigeons,
                        the Owl
                        & Sparrows
                                    —To See To It!
            that Whales sailed safely
                        to the Open Waters
                                        of
                                their Homes,
                                            iF
                    Every Child had its own.

122

The Pigeon Squawk

All Pigeons are not
               the Same!
O Yes!
        They all have their
                sleek grey necks
        which glisten green
                        against the sun
But some
      trust human beings,
   While others give
                their side-long
                        glances
        of mistrust,
                having thus
                    no doubt
                        , Observed
            How, even children
                chase them
                            —sca t te   ri   n g
           after their parents
                        ,old aged
                            lonely people
            have tossed spiked
                bread crumbs
                        laced with
            granulated
                    glass
                        & mirrors
                            in the grass
   And cars run over
                them
                    ,while crossing
            simple-minded streets
                            ,though bicycles
                                    cut lines
                            through them

                                        as just as well
                        in smalltown parks
                                quite indiscrete;
While famous mayors
                of famous cities
        sign ordinary ordinances
                against annoyances
                        ,which send them
                                to their ovens
                                        ,because
                        ,Science says
                                they spread
                                        dreaded diseases;
                                                ,though
                                Old Ladies
                                        love them
                                        for their memories . . .

Some Pigeons like to
                Watch
        the World
                        ,and having once
                                been human
                                        beings ,themselves
        They cannot stand
                        their smells
        so they sit
                on window sills
                        & watch
                the daily destruction
                                of human life
                                        ,and trees
                        give way
                                to highways
                        and purchases
                                        of perchless
                                        condominiums

                        124

,though
           ,if left alone
       Pigeons would rather
                           ,nonchalantly
           sit on statues
               against the law
                           and other
               monuments
           of men
               and do Their Thing
                                   ,which is
                   Actually
                   what Everybody
                               including you, &
                                   maybe me
                           most like to do
But that is
           Private and
       Pigeons are
           Public birds
                   who
               flaunt their
                   Pubic hairs
           ,and therefore why
           we resent them
                   so . . .

Artista Cubano

"Oye verde, oye azul."

Years ago Pepe came from the fields
to Havana, swept *el taller,* watched
men mix yellow rustle of hibiscus
with black pad of cat stalking its shadow.

"Oye verde, oye azul."

He walked streets hearing
the blare of a girl's skirt, whirl red,
purling of light on a dove's creamy feathers,
clamor of the island's canary sun.

"Oye verde, oye azul."

The men watched his eyes
stroke paint, lost in his listening, begin
to mix the sough of sea pines with the lisp
of waves, swirl aquamarine.

"Oye verde, oye azul."

He hardly heard money's loud-mouth noise,
its purrs, the tic-toc of hard boots marching
down streets, the loudspeakers blasting:
yanqui imperialistas, yanqui imperialistas,

Che's flags flapping in the heat,
bar music rippling down the street

from days when Papa H.
strolled with his *compañeros* downing daquiris.

"Oye verde, oye azul."

Curly hair gray now but still shirtless,
he sweats over his work, says he loves it,
all he knows how to do, slides stone on stone
and a face appears, sea eyes, a blue he can float in.

"Oye verde, oye azul."

Sly Woman

The woman who hides from me is sly, but careless
in her invisibility. She moves through my rooms at ease,
rubbing lemon oil into wood tables, cleaning
kitchen counters with a damp cloth, but I see her signs:
half-empty cup of tea, open book,
cluster of rocks and pods, pitcher of wildflowers.

I again begin my search; room to room I stalk
her like I'd stalk my daughter's cat when it hid
to sleep inside. I listen with my skin. She is sly,
but doesn't know I feel her move with no sound down my
    hall.

I push the swinging door, and there she is, caught
in the act, her kitchen hands humming so
she doesn't hear my breath. How small and peaceful
she seems, slicing carrots and cucumber in the sun,
that old rhythm, the drumming of a knife,
sliced circles of sun and moon, the slow pleasure
of a woman who now cooks only for herself.
My hands reach to grab her dress, and make her look at me
and see this is *my* house, but my hands feel only a breeze
strumming my fingers with its song.

GEAN MORENO

Amantes Sin Tiempo

—after Mario Carreno's painting

Not even time can rearrange your face.
Naked, not body, you arrive

on this landscape that un-makes itself
to become a wasteland populated by totems

of limbs. Fleshless animals keep vigilance
for the face, Hamlet's seeds vast

in the clay prairies. Night melts
the clock's hands and our traits.

Yours run down your chin. Mine consolidate
into a stalactite of nerve and flesh.

The two of us instilled in our Spring
attire allow love, more dagger

than emotion, to graze our countenance
and then devour the eyes, the nose,

the lips. Tonight, surrendering again,
we evoke the petaled ambush. Lost,

we forget its thorn and all the other
scenes that play in memory's theater.

Memory is face; face
is fear. Adam never had eyes.

Lorca in Hell

Telephone wires thread
the city together
as you travel through
the East River and the Bronx,
among desperate children,
their faces stained
by coal and their bellies
bare for your green looks.
Nothing was familiar,
except the translated verses
of Whitman that you read
in the **Residencia** in Madrid.
In your dorm at Columbia
a gun slept on the top drawer
of your desk awaiting
the call of your temple.
Sevilla and Cadiz
were old yellow memories.
The Queensborough
and Hudson were real,
and the paranoid homosexuals
with fevers of fans in public squares
that seduced the children of the gutter.
But you weren't corrupted. You wanted
the faggot that was pure.

The industry came and swept away
the fields of Andalusia
that had been replicated
on the soil of the New World.
You knew that the jobless
would be carried off
by the roaring current
of a river of caskets.
You knew the children
would never sleep again,

they would never want to be river,
or cloud, or fern.
You knew that your **romances**
would not suffice
to find the New York of life,
the angel it has hidden in its cheek.
By now, the gypsies had vanished
and you were alone in the metropolis,
where a death dressed in velvet sought you
through the wilderness of brick and glass.

Repetitions

One doesn't have to be
eighty
to write about endings.
There are autumns of all ages.
This one I'm going through
is only thirtysomething.

I'd love to be cynical.
I'd love to make fun
of my Cuban American angst,
of my ethnic tragicomedy.
Baby Boomer and Yuca,
Cubiche, Yuckie *con mojo*.
But I can't
This situation is
a serious situation.
Although there's nothing new
about my plight:
I've laughed so many times
at this gray sky and these
dying trees.
And yet today those trees
and that sky are my companions,
not my invention.
As real as death.

Como la misma muerte.

One doesn't have to be
eighty
to write about repetitions.

Repetitions happen at any age.
And they are always painful.
It hurts to have to wait
for spring. Again.
It hurts to describe
an autumn day without you,
these same old leaves.
This new repetition.
Again.

Summer of the Body

When the Filipino doctor,
soft-spoken and fatherly,
inquires,
Are you close to your grandfather?
(Or did he say *were* you close?)
And he tells me of the necessary end.
(Perhaps he said "inevitable.")
The NO CODE.
The usual resuscitation that
the almost-dead man will not receive.
There's no point, says the doctor.
Because sooner or later
(any second now)
we all must endure
the summer of the body.
No one is exempt.

We are prepared,
I guess.
We have already bought
the burial plot and
we have chosen the lettering
for his tombstone.

(We were so pleased
to see the graveyard;
the tombs were hidden
under welcoming grass.)
We'll offer him a wake,
his *velorio*.
And we will dress him in a guayabera.
I guess we'll do
What has to be done.

Abuelo's hands,
his massive fingers,
still warm.
His skin cannot bear another shot.
That's why we have this perfumed cream,
clean sheets and feather pillows,
this cool air,
for him.

Summers of the body can be merciless.

Mariano, the Air

I believe today is Friday.
On this train headed for Madrid,
I'm thinking of Mariano.
Driven mad by the memory,
I remember Mariano.
He took care of me.
He worried about me.
"*Cuanto te quiero*," we said.

On this train headed for Madrid
I'm reliving our fantasy:
We were childhood friends.

133

(Mariano in Segovia
with his *amiguito;*
both leaning against
the front door of a church,
reluctant to enter,
freezing to death,
kept barely alive
by their desire.)

I realize this now:
It was Mariano who made
the first move.
I didn't seek him out.
(I never look for them.)

What do I do now, on this train,
to get Mariano out of me?
Breathe again. Deeply.
Or maybe this is life:
running, desperate
for oxygen.

Mariano, the air.

Frutas

Growing up in Miami any tropical fruit I ate
could only be a bad copy of the Real Fruit of Cuba.
Exile meant having to consume false food,
and knowing it in advance. With joy
my parents and grandmother would encounter
Florida-grown mameyes and caimitos at the market.
At home they would take them out of the American bag
and describe the taste that I and my older sister
would, in a few seconds, be privileged to experience
for the first time. We all sat around the table
to welcome into our lives this football-shaped,
brown fruit with the salmon-colored flesh
encircling an ebony seed. "Mamey,"
my grandmother would say with a confirming nod,
as if repatriating a lost and ruined name.
Then she bent over the plate,
slipped a large slice of mamey into her mouth,
then straightened in her chair and, eyes shut,
lost herself in comparison and memory.
I waited for her face to return with a judgment.
"No, not even the shadow of the ones back home."
She kept eating more calmly,
and I began tasting the sweet and creamy pulp
trying to raise the volume of its flavor
so that it might become a Cuban mamey. "The good
Cuban mameyes didn't have primaveras," she said
after the second large gulp, knocking her spoon
against a lump in the fruit and winking.
So at once I erased the lumps in my mental mamey.
I asked her how the word for "spring"
came to signify "lump" in a mamey. She shrugged.
"Next you'll want to know how we lost a country."

Mulata

*Afirmaban los egipcios que era fecundada al ser atravesada
por un rayo de sol.*

—Jose Lezama Lima, *Las Eras Imaginarias*

The shadow inside the flame will be human
for a while longer. Alcohol's bouquet is awash
in the incense of flesh, silk, and bone.
Only Buddhist monks and Cuban mulatas die like this.
Jilted and pregnant, it's either the whorehouse
or death by fire. By any means but fire
is the preferred way because it cleanses much
as the sun ignites the birth exhausted cow
to produce a last calf in Lezama's reading
of Herodotus among the Egyptians.

Who can imagine an era, who can help doing so?
Our lives toss on the surf that gulps the thinnest shore,
break amid a gallop of shells and the atomic shadows
each towering kernel casts. Some minute beast beneath
the sweet desert that frames the world's two selves
must think the weight of a lover's flesh
something other than love, must plot
to escape amid pathless ochres flowing like thick
air, beloved element in the hourglass' waist.

In fact, her figure was often compared to an hourglass.
The mulata would dress modestly in light yellows
and blues to walk the gauntlet of **piropos**
jeered by men made horny by duty and the tropic sun
on her way to work, a visit, or mass. Her special love
was window shopping. Only the lewdest **piropo**
could pull her like a wave from a dance of plenty
with those painless citizens. At times she felt
a pug-fingered hand lighting on her ass
like foam on sand, and she would jolt or, lately,
just brush it off like a fly
before wandering away in calm, arousing sways.
The dancers would freeze until her next visit.

136

Her lover was white, probably married, twice her age,
short, hurried, and cheaper than she had expected.
She lived in a **solar,** a tenement, in **La Habana Vieja.**
On their designated Wednesday afternoons
he would shed his **guayabera** while she was still
struggling with the elastics and buckles
that held the paling silk to her legs.
He would linger in his undershirt and boxer shorts
during her ritual and let his cigar tip downward
from his teeth like a compass needle mistaking
her frail ankles for north. He felt reassured
by the tacky boleros oozing from her nightstand radio
and by her bedroom shrine to **Santa Barbara.**
The candles flickered amid apples and roses,
and red-caped **chango** guarded their screw with a sword.
During his mount the national metaphors for sex
would possess and confuse him, making him hungry.
His chest hairs swirled on her syrupy **mameyes,**
her lips became slices of **guayaba,**
and only American tourists order **papaya**
instead of "bomb fruit" before blushing waitresses.
Hunger and the corner cafe would make him come fast.

After being stood up two Wednesdays in a row
her mother shook her head, "He's gone, all right,
and how will we pay the landlord."
"Not all of him is gone," she recited to herself
inventing a line worthy of a **bolero** or a radio **novela.**
She tugged her abdomen and, miraculously,
another heroic line would come, "Panic would grow
faster than any child within her."
It would be a male, she knew it, and unlike her
he would pass for white, would become
a doctor and travel and strip those mannequins
for her with his wallet. All the **novelas**
have tragic plots but happy outcomes.
No one would accuse him, "And where's your grandmother?"
while pointing a grin at his African nose.

They had met in front of the windows at **El Encanto,**
the biggest store in Havana. She was transfixed
by the double skirts just in from France,
he was carrying a **Mariquita Perez** doll for **Reyes.**
It was January in Havana. He could take her
to the colored beach where his infidelity
could go safely witnessed. One afternoon
he would go well beyond the fondlings
with which he had seasoned her like a ham,
and beneath the cheap frill of palm trees
he would sign her naked ass on the sand.

He had left for Miami with his wife
and daughter. She couldn't bear
the rallied screams of the Revolution
or its **milicianos** who flooded
Havana from the countryside and saw her
as part of the spoils. **El Encanto**
had been set ablaze. She dreamt
the mannequins trapped in the inferno
the night she raced out of the **solar**
amid the most inhuman cries,
like those of birth.

Carlos Alfonzo

Who said you were free and why did you believe
it? The pierced tongue dances with its nail,
hums the melody toward which it moves like grief.

The forms in your paintings clash like leaves
in God's dark night, who first learned to fail
daring us: be free if you can believe

your dramas are but the echoes of my dreams.
His orders calm the wind and cure the sail
on its harmonious journey to the rim of grief.

Abjured horizon, vanished points in which we leave
found ruins to make our own from the pale
rations of freedom and in ourselves believe,

with ourselves dance hiddenly like tides with reefs
breaking hull, heart and reason in a wail
deaf till music, like a journey makes a map live

that was but drawn dead purpose. Though broken, brief,
your flesh dance with knives guides us as we rail
against freedoms called to order, a life believed
instead of sung. The death of journeys, our only grief.

The First Rock and Roll Song of 1970

The unemployed sky above the clouds
that have replaced the hair on the buildings
Whose tenants live and look forward
to the last supper on the lost calendar
They swallowed years before they were born
and tormented by the consolidated edison grass
Who never took dancing lessons from the sun

The wind hits the clothing lines
secondhand underwear take off into eternity
The owner panics and jumps out the window
to look for them because he will not be able
To face his friends again if he gets buried
without those underwears he has not finished
Paying for yet. Last night a teenage mother

Put an airmail stamp on the forehead
of her illegitimate son and threw him out
The window to make it on his own in this
cruel world. The woman pleaded insane
To the authorities when she was arrested
and was sentenced to night school to finish
High School and become a full time waitress

When the war is over and the motion
picture industry shows how america won again
there will be nobody in the audience.
Little boys and girls shout at each other:
"My father's coffin makes your father's coffin
Look like a box of matches." The fee to pee
will be discontinued. Shaved head morticians

Dance with their favorite dead politicians
and the next president of the united states
Will learn how to read the help wanted ads

Ode to Witch Liberty

Rooster feathers replace the wings
Of fallen angels from Purgatory
To make them look young once again
Ready to crow at the break of dawn
And reverse the night into daylight
After the external nocturnal flight
Into the final feelings of her arms
That turns love on and off and on
Until eternity is within reach of
A never to be forgotten moment
And evidence of after life passion
Materializes before the naked eye—
Beware! She is wise & unpredictable
Holds you tight to keep you loose,
Her heart tells the truth & nothing
But! Until the honeymoon is over
And you will never again be sober
Or drink from the same strange river
Of times that misplaced your vanity
And left you far away from yourself
To dance with a human space race
Among the bright and darker lights
Of her perfumed conceptual bedroom
Where lit candles handle darkness
Extremely well when there are no lies
To tell the comfort death receives
Where the missing persons loiter
Talking absentmindedly to themselves
Until a ripe coconut from a palm tree

They no longer remember climbing
Drops on the center of the skull
And they briefly feel witch liberty
Smiling as the spirit leaves the body
From one dead vagrant to new hobo
Infant tender & mild & wild & destined
To misplace many things in life
Because she will never be the wife
Of he or anybody who tries to modify
Her down to earth psychic powers—
And she only accepts frozen flowers
From gardens where it snows constantly,
Oh it is there her fires come from
To decorate her soul with dark secrets
From flames that forget your name
As you remember who you never were
Inside thoughts of frogs and lizards
That chased a snake off the roof
And it fell into a lake of ironic soup
That cures and kills you for sure
To keep your dreams inside your head
So that they may never have to end
And you can assume Witch Liberty
And you are an inseparable extension
Of the same Island reserved 4 silence
As long as you pledge high allegiance
To your imagination—she will follow
To make you feel like a real king
Destined to become her slave any day
As fact & fantasy becomes the same
& you better not mention her name
While she is occupied meditating
Or she will surely drive you insane
& chase you onto a midair collision
With unidentifiable flying objects,
And you will never again be able
To make another round table rise—
With Liberty just wants the world

for a friend NOT overprotective lover
Companion circus ring leader hermit
In old clothes compatible to Zen—
She fell off the highest wire once
Upon a few mundane misunderstandings
About who said Let there be light!
Her heart cannot be broken twice
So Poet become your own fatal wife
If what you fear most is insecurity!
She is sure and unsure of everything
Now that she knows where the wind
Goes when it doesn't blow in the air,
If you stare She will be there
To let you watch her comb her hair
At twilight time in all her thoughts
Of how the world ended a long time ago
Because no one alive believed in magic
And so the sun had no reason to rise
Inside the eyes of sleepy children—
Rain & thunder & occasional lightning
Accompanied the dilemma of being
Realistic as head falls off shoulder
And is never seen or heard from again
At the end of the endless sexy pause
In a nightmare about happy endings—
We are only pretending—Aren't we?
Hell No! Heaven yes! Replies Witch
Of Liberty for all who are present
The following amnesia induced morning
While it's still dark enough to see
And you have to go and keep coming
'Til you meet again to propose love
& marriage & stability & boredom
& disappointment til death survives
The crisis in a divorce from life
For making her your personal wife
Without ever becoming her friend—
And once again she will refuse to be

The bottom of your missing deep blue
Spirit sea of sacred contradictions
That deliver you not from evil ever
So that you may never be able to
Imagine a short cut to paradise
At the entrance of her third eye
The eye that sees everything clear
And knows nothing about anything
Until all the lights are turned off

Nighttime Sunshine Mind Game

did she tell you
as she read the cards
that your heart is
a foreign country
without borders to impede
love at first sight
on the last day of the universe?

did she tell you
that a secret overt admirer
who prefers to remain anonymous
all the nights of his illusions
detects eternity in eyes
that wear your delicate body?

did she tell you
he is constantly thinking
about constantly telling you
he constantly thinks about you
when he's pretending to sleep
after doubting another vision
of how he ended up lost
in the desert of his thoughts?

did she tell you
about an endless daydreamer
who spends all his spare time
fantasizing about your after-life
indicating that you will never
be absent from his inner conflict
long after you cease being fine
to then become fantastic!

did she tell you
he is capable of necrophilia
should you sleep late
the following morning
after finally meeting yourself
over the somewhere else rainbow
within walking distance from
a satisfaction that never comes

did she mention
a familiar undiscovered garden
where the flowers at all hours
are incredible and impossible
& the sublime season shines
in an everlasting summertime
inside of mirrors the night stares into

where the living stays easy
& ghost stories are fascinating
& the wine is victoriously red
& the history of eternal miseries
continues to repeat itself slowly?

did she tell you this?
did your finger tips tremble
as you suddenly remember meeting
in the perfumed valley of shadows
where the moon stays full forever
in a slow dream of fast dancing
& eternal romancing before dawn?

did she tell you to beware?
did she tell you to despair?
did she tell you to prepare
for clues leading to evidence
of immortality shortly after
the romance with death ends?

and last but not least
did she tell you that you have
the right to remain silent
or become a stranger yourself
aboard a spaceless ship that must sink
into your heart with him there
during an amazing discovery
of passion 2 personal 4 details

did she tell you this?
did she tell you all of this?
and if she didn't tell you this
then he is telling you this
& this is what he is telling you!

Aye Que Maria Felix (or Maria Was No Virgin)

I am Maria Felix
done up in black;
soft wool clinging
lace collar high
and plunging backline
lower than the
San Joaquin Valley.
Attitude all the way
arched eyebrow
arrogant tilt of head.
Men swoon meekly at my feet.
Mexicana to the max
Molcajete Mama
calling the shots
shooting from the hips,
full moon of womanhood
casting shadows over
unsuspecting hearts.
Wide wingspan of spell
over the strongest men.
Que teatro
swishing feminine
to the backlash of salvation.
Perfumanes rise
from the thick sensuality
of night's mysterious swell.
Who is this woman
that crosses my path
and leads me to unknown worlds of intrigue?
Is she me, or a Channel 34 mirage?
Que susto to discover

the aching hearts of men
and find the stark loneliness
of their dreams embedded
in the illusion of sexuality.
Maria would peal that
spit-in-your-eye-cabron laughter
y dar la media vuelta
into the obscurity
of her own heart.
Head held high
and high heels digging
into the cruelty
of love's passion.
I only laugh into the wine
of a dubious power
and find refuge from passion's
cruel illusion.
Ave Maria
Y que viva la mujer!

Post-Colonial Contemplations

I

The world grows smaller
and our faces larger
this strange proximity
makes us uneasy neighbors.
The centuries have held
like walls around us
the oceans—wet borderlands
have floated dark diseases
into the veins of confused decades.
Iron fists have punched holes
into the stunned face
of each bruised epoch.

Now we must face the other
now we must face ourselves.
The days like anger
have disappeared
into the vanity of each second,
our time has been enslaved like this
for 500 years of alternating servitudes.
We have bowed before too many false gods
and our prayers have made slaves of us.

II

I have a thousand gods
inside me dancing
a goddess in every room,
I am a born again pagan
whirling the sins of the world
on my nose.
Jester, fool, mad victim
of inappropriate appropriations.
My acrobatic karmas bounce
like noisy children
off the walls of my inner cities
I run with echoes
that call me many names
I call my gods many names
we remain anonymous—however—
on a stage called the universe
and not even 500 can steal that away.
Not even 500 years can erode that spirit
or extinguish the namelessness
of each face that has faced
the uncertainty of namelessness.

III

Translating soul
into the language of numbers
is a treacherous grammar

filled with false punctuation
of sliced skin that burns
a bright pink
in blue eyes
capitalizing on every letter
of each dark image it re-creates.
People passages have been held captive
inside the parentheses of a greedy discourse.
We have lost our language
and hold tight
like the clenched fist
of a fussing infant
to that which keeps us mute.
What century shall loosen our tongues
and give us back our words?
When will the other know the other
enough to leave the scab alone?
It is too silent here among us
and there is need for a bold
new language.
The dialect of derelicts
is the seed of new expression
articulating on the edge
of old desires
for times that never were
and reproducing on fears
of what may never come.
Let poets and madwomen
speak this language to you.
It will resound in the strangeness
of utterances
that are all too familiar.

Poem Written During One of My Yearly Visits from California

There is an old song about the river

I first heard long ago,

that I've carried inside me ever since:

"I was born by the river

and just like the river

I've been running ever since."

There is another song,

about a man whose life, like the river

continually runs away from him:

"Soy como el agua del rio,

todo se me va en correr."

Perhaps my life ran counter to my shadow.

At times my shadow fled from me.

Strange how you look around one day

and you're home again, for a while,

never more than a while, and you realize

that somehow you made your way to the sea

and that you had come home to understand

how your life ran and the river runs.

Don Chuey

In the United States Don Chuey is officially Joseph Henry.

A name he considers an insult.

Long ago his father left Mexico to work in the U.S.

The railroad led to rural Minnesota,

and in time he sent for his wife,

who was pregnant with Don Chuey.

She arrived one night ready to deliver,

and Don Chuey's father set out immediately.

When he finally found a doctor

he also found him unwilling,

hosting a party in his honor.

Don Chuey's father pleaded and pleaded,

but the doctor refused, then finally gave in,

on the condition that, this being his birthday,

the child, if a boy, be named after him.

Kid Hielero

He had a couple of fights
But they didn't add up.
Kid Hielero became a name for the bars,

A name for a laugh
As if who could believe it
Looking at him now,

Or it was just a name to remember
The way one talked about radio shows,
The Shadow, and who could remember

The man's real name, Lamont Cranston—
As if a radio guy could have a real name—
But it's what we said anyway,

And didn't think about it.

Anyone from Nogales in the Fifties
Would remember it—
Well they'd remember it but maybe not him:

Kid Hielero took his name
From the old ice house
Right on Grand Avenue coming in,

The *hielero*, where he worked for a while
The way everyone worked for a while
At some point in life.

Small towns work like this.

The ice chutes used to pass over
The road through town
And ice water dripped like rain

On the cars underneath.
It could have been a car wash
And everybody could have been rich

But it wasn't, and they weren't.
These were the days when the railroad
Needed ice

For the cabbages and the lettuce,
The masses of sugar beets.
It was in the days when small towns,

These small towns,
You know what I mean,
Needed themselves.

Kid Hielero died
In another time altogether,
Suffering the invention of cancer.

When it happened
All he wanted was watermelon.
It was a fancy hospital

And the nurses got some
Even though it was winter, September.
I remember they said they were ready

For this. They said
Somebody who's dying,
They always want watermelon.

It's the women from Mexico
In the kitchen, they knew
Right from the beginning

This would happen.
Not for him, of course, not specifically,
Just for people like him.

So they freeze a little in the summer.
They said the women in the kitchen said
It's from another time

And it's all I could say, too,
Yes, I said.
I think that's true,

It's from another time.
I think that's what you say,
And I think it helps.

Kid Hielero watched the World Series
And ate the watermelon
And died,

And he left me his daughter
For a wife.
It happened quick

So that everyone forgot
About the watermelon,
Just like The Shadow's real name.

But there it is
And I don't know what you do with it,
This knowing about what the dying

Want to eat.
You remember it sometimes
But not everyone else does.

You just remember it
Because there you are with it
Every time you eat watermelon.

Combing My Hair in the Hall

Each time the doors to her room were opened
a little of the gathered light left
and the small room became blacker
moving somewhere in a twilight toward night.
And then a little of the light left
not her room, but her falling face
as each time she opened the smaller doors
that were her wooden eyes.
She talked only with her mouth then
no longer with the force of her wild eyes
and that, too, made her less,
each word leaving her now
as the way her firm bones had abandoned her.
Then she spoke with her woman's hands
only, no words left, then only with her smell
which once had been warm, tortillitas,
or like sugar breads just made.
In the half-words of our other language,
in the language of the new world
of which she had had time to show me
only half, I tried to speak to her,
to fill her up, to tell her the jokes
of the day, and fill her too much
with laughing, fill her fat like she had been,
and my brother Tomas tried too, we
touched her, were made to touch her,
we kissed her even, lips trying
to quickly press back the something
as children even we could feel
but whose name she had not told us,
and as we kissed her, bent and kissed her,
we could smell her, I shivered, and we both
breathed out hard when we had to
put our lips there, like later we would learn
to drink pulque and be men, trying even that
to push her back into herself.

But she was impatient with us, or smarter,
or quicker, so that we did smell her,
she made us, and taste the insides of her,
and take her in small parts with us
but not like drink, not like men—instead,
like the smell of bread taken by the heart
into the next day, or into dreams.
Every night she wanted to be young again
as she slept there on her bed
and in the night, in the minute she could
no longer talk, and did not smell, or wake,
she was, again, young: we
opened our mouths
and asked words about her, cried
bits of ourselves out through our eyes,
each sigh expelled, each tear,
each word said now making us,
us less, not her, each word gone
making room in ourselves for her,
so that one day, again, she laughs hard,
a Thursday, four voices stronger, five,
laughs at something none of us understands,
standing there, comb in hand, laughs
at something silly, or vain, or the story
of the six sisters of mercy, perhaps, she
just laughs looking at all of her new faces
full in the mirror at the end of the hall.

Diana Rivera

Poetry of the Holy Water

comes like a chameleon, placed
mysteriously by larger hands
between leaves and colors in the tuft
of earth,
a holy chameleon
cleverly, gently placed
by God, as two
humans meet:
cell to cell,
eye to eye, that endless
channel of depth and gratitude,
that sacred process
of the macro in the micro—
water, love—
infinitesimal
pure reactions:
division, or static calmness
(our movements perhaps naturalized
in the single, ever-moving point of peace)
or to choose dis/ease,
the entering into the pits and maladies
of our endless sorrows
through our bodies which are
really our souls,
because really we are all,
those we are with,
all which we see—
by giving pain we feel pain,
by giving love we feel love—
in the smallest tear perhaps the cure,
the relief from the small poison,

as water is everywhere
where there is life—
with forgiveness
a holy seed
sprouts calmly.

from **Bird Language**

1.

. . .
In the gray dusk,
in my silence,
I look out the window.
A bird in the brush of lilacs
scuffles, shifts and shakes
the crispy leaves; it flies across
back and forth,
busily, noisily, but not singing;
for a long stretch of time it scurries in
the shilly-shallying lilacs—
this grace-speckled, dim dark oval
over all the leaves which speak.
From behind
rises the sly, light-shaded morbid grayness
of the dying sun.
Could this, I wonder
be the same huge, plump
bluejay
I saw today in the yard near the lilacs!
It seems to follow me, needs to find me,
it rings its bell,
it is a blue
holy
spirit behind the brambles.

I think, regardless
of the windowpane which broke today in our bedroom,
of the near-impossibility of the act,
of the tiny glass speckles that sprang in the air, in the
                                                    (fury

and carelessness of younger hands;
how the glass flung
lightly across his face, how he,
cursing quietly, lifted edged fragments, and I
loved him with my faraway spirit
of near desolation,
and fighting
the mending,
I could see loving
his young, tender
unflawed livingness
kissing the unseen life,
the physical, spirited life.

Now, seeing the last speckles, I sweep the floor.
When I return after placing the dustpan back in its dark
                                                    (closet,
the bird spirit is gone,
the branches are silent,

the knowingness of all
the words I have not heard
descends upon me, like
a flame.

I remember how they used to speak in tongues,
the apostles,
like these birds, jiggling and twittering like
brown maracas
singing in Spanish, German and Greek—
a silence, suddenly fluid
with an array of different
temperamental voices.

160

I remember how
there were many sounds,
how a bird smacked another with a giant kiss
on its left cheek,
sounds tinted
burnt yellow, pale rose, scorched blue,
how, afterwards, the scarecrow
frightened away the delicate
wings that trembled with voices.
I remember how they used to speak in tongues,
their love bond
surpassing the unflinching barriers of language,
they, us
years back, thousands
of years back, and only then
was it all silken. Now birds
fly all over and cannot find me,
speak of a thousand glossy notes and a thousand glossy
forms of love.

2.

The crissal thrasher
tumbles through air
where love is light,
tempting, forbidden
because the Laws of Birds state so:
How often do they weep?
How much can they endure?
They tumble through their heavy branches
dizzy, blind, stuffed with cankerworms
to their guts, for hunger's all
they can think of,
and live for,

and they Peep because they have forgotten
how to Weep
                    and they Peep & Peep

their little bodies breaking apart,
filled up to their tiny muscular hearts
with splitting seeds.
Their pink eyes
tear in song

because they have forgotten

how to cry,
and their feathers are dying,
and their feathers are snowed and tangled.
They perch their long winters alone
in someone else's wooden, painted house,
spine knotted,
their tiny pearly eyes
breaking.

And when love weeps the loss of its own loss
and calls the peewit lapwing in despair,
the lapwing, flapping, sings:

Comeback!

the waterhen's eye
slowly rises from deep water
alert, in Quacks
foreshadowing

the shrugging tug of loneliness.
The body, which was sleeping,
awakes again into the carnal passage of its presence
and, as it awakens, lapwings' and waterhens' tiny feet and
(once

desperate beaks
create the everlasting
periodic ripples
of love eternal.

Death of the Lady Slipper

It came to an end, the rose of his intellect
flew to meet the soul of his emotions.
A crystal clear delusion took hold of his spirit.

His eyes recalled every inch of light,
line, shadow, form,
memorized the skeleton he could see under my skin,
the clitoral crease in the center of my petal,
the oval perfect, tongue-shaped swirls
crushed under his footsteps,
before he raped my patch of forest.

Concave forms, soft curves come back—
you once were, I once was, you inside,
my body calling yours, calling,
earth! sky! petal!
I gripping you tight, holding you in, forming one
inner flower.
Not letting go we loved wrecklessly,
I swam on your body, over your erotic motions,
your face buried in the darkness of the flower inside me,
your earth under and over the crease of my petal.
Having to let me go must be punishment from the gods.
    Nearby
the beavers carved the totems of death.

Tearing down trees for more sun and grass
the brightness ate me up, dried me up—I
who once thrived in the moist half-shadows
small, translucent viscosity
so alive in self-intimacy under pines by the lake.
As I die
others die in a chain of events.

Oh, dear love
dear beauty, regained for a moment,

lost again for infinity, as the terror
of a broken thought.
Under lakewaters, a revolution of blood and petals.
Her ache was the thrum of a hummingbird
not finding a single culprit.

You extinct, I extinct—
he betrayed her with his intellect.
He took her moisture away, the chilled lapping of leaves
that fanned her,
the flora which gave form to her breath.

Lady slipper,
language of flowers,
divinely conceived spaces
scattered as small graces—
your untouched, virginal cavities
in love with cool, wet earth, orchid moss, humus dreams,
once lived
dispersed in meanders of half-shadowed,
half-lit habitats.

The wet scent of your petals lingers
near the damp darkness of ferns.
where, centered in feeble pistils,
your heart melted.
where your silken skin shriveled
as puckered crepe paper.
Your last breath released, mountains
cry in your absence.
No trees, no leaves survived
the killer sun,
the rational acquisitions of greedy men.

Self-Portrait with Thorn Necklace and Hummingbird (1940)

The signs of age around my eyes
that look tired
even my eyebrows are quiet.

I wanted to adorn myself once again.
Last night I had a dream that I was
looking for a new outfit
but I didn't have the money.

I found something beautiful
hanging on a rack, still dreaming
I knew I could not afford it
but, I wanted to look beautiful in it.

So instead I paint myself with a crown
of braids and lavender ribbons,
two butterfly combs in my hair.

I am still not happy.
There seems to be a necklace of dried
thorns choking me. A dead hummingbird
hangs as a medallion. A charm.
Its wings spread open, stiff.

My pet monkey at my shoulder,
grooming itself, snapping lice dead.
A black panther at my other shoulder
stalking, waiting for its prey.

My neck and the hummingbird
bleed.

The Dream

The dream exists only in myself.
While I sleep the ivy plants
grow around me, enfold my blankets,
sheets, the green grows out from
my hair.

My eyes can't see what is real.
The dream floats around
my bed. The mahogany bed posts
hold up the canopy where a
skeleton rests above me.

Perhaps I am dying. The skeleton lies
on her side,
holds a bouquet of lavender flowers,
rests her head on a pillow,
her leg bones separated
and held together by cables and wires. The ivy wrapped
    around
my neck.

Everything floats in the clouds.
The vision suspended in space.
There is no sound. The green
muffles my throat.

Self-Portrait with Cropped Hair (1940)

The epitome of woman
is to dress in a man's suit and
sit with open legs
in a masculine posture
and still be beautiful.

Holding the scissors
that just cut the long strands
hair fallen everywhere

Like Delilah
I wish to erase memory.

The bitter taste of you
still on my tongue.

LUIS J. RODRÍGUEZ

They Come to Dance

An aged, bondo-scarred Buick
pushes dust around its wheels
as it slithers up Brooklyn Avenue
toward La Tormenta, bar and dance club.

The Buick pulls up to clutter
along a cracked sidewalk
beneath a street lamp's yellow luminance.
A man and a woman, in their late 30s,
pour out of a crushed side door.

They come to dance.

The man wears an unpressed suit and baggy pants:
K-Mart specials.
She is overweight
in a tight blue dress.
The slits up the side
reveal lace and panty hose.

They come with passion-filled bodies,
factory-torn like *ropa vieja*.
They come to dance the workweek away
as a soft rain begins to buffet
the club's steamed windows.

Women in sharp silk dresses and harsh,
painted-on makeup crowd the entrance.
Winos stare at the women's flight across
upturned streets
and up wooden stairs.

Men in slacks and cowboy shirts
or cheap polyester threads
walk alone or in pairs.

"*¡Oye compa, que pues!*
Aqui, no más, de oquis . . ."

Outside La Tormenta's doors
patrons line up to a van dispensing tacos
while a slightly opened curtain
reveals figures gyrating
to a beat bouncing off strobe-lit walls.

They come to dance
and remember
the way flesh feels flush
against a cheek
and how a hand opens slightly,
shaped like a seashell,
in the small
of a back.

They come to dance
and forget
the pounding hum
of an assembly line,
while the boss' grating throat
tells everyone to go back to work
over the moans of a woman
whose finger dangles
in a glove.

They come to dance:
Former peasants. Village kings.
City squatters. High-heeled princesses.

The man and woman lock the car doors
and go through La Tormenta's weather-stained

curtain leading into
curling smoke.

Inside the Buick are four children.
They press their faces
against the water-streaked glass
and cry through large eyes;
mirrors of a distant ocean.

Bethlehem No More

(For Bruce S.)

Bethlehem Steel's
shift-turn whistles
do not blast out
in Maywood anymore.

Mill workers no longer congregate
at Slauson Avenue bars
on pay day.

Bethlehem's soaking pits
are frigid now.

Mill families,
once proud and comfortable,
now gather for unemployment checks
or food.

Bethlehem,
I never thought you would be missed.
When we toiled under the girders,
we cursed your name.

But you were bread on the table;
another tomorrow.

My babies were born
under the Bethlehem health plan.
My rent was paid
because of those long and humid
days and nights.

I recall being lowered
into oily and greasy pits
or standing unsteady
on two-inch beams
thirty feet in the air
and wondering if I would survive
to savor another weekend.

I recall my fellow workers
who did not survive—
burned alive from caved-in furnace roofs
or severed in two by burned red steel rods—
while making your production quotas.

But Bethlehem you are no more.
We have made you rich;
rich enough to take our toil
and invest it elsewhere.

Rich enough
to make us poor again.

Deathwatch

1.

There is a room in the old house
where the dead sleep,
not dead like without life,
dead like winter,
breathing the moments in
but decay everywhere.

In spring, blossoms burn with color
but each wrinkle, every new invasion
of gray over black on your head
is only a fraction step
in your lifelong demise.

Living with you, Pop,
was like being on a deathwatch.
A slow dying of day, a candle flickering.
What of the man who taught high school
in *Ciudad Juárez*, wrote biology books
and stormed the rigid government-
controlled system there—
the one who dared new life?

Where have you been, my father?
You were always escaping,
always a faint memory of fire,
a rumor of ardor;
sentenced to leaving
but never gone.

2.

He will never understand
the silence that drove me to the alley,
that kept me tied
to the gravel of deadly play;
why I wanted to die, just to know him.

One day I got drunk with a work crew
and everyone talked about their
imprisoned dads, their junkie dads, their no-dads
and I said I had a dad, but I never heard him
say love, never heard him say son,
and how I wished he wasn't my dad,
but the others yelled back:
How can you judge?
How do you know what he had to do
to be there! Could I do better?
Could I walk in his shoes
and pretend a presence?

3.

He wasn't always there.
Lisa died as an infant
after accidentally eating *chicharrones*
he sold on cobblestoned streets in Mexico.
Seni was abandoned and left with his mom.
A story tells of a young Seni who answered the door
to a stranger, wet from a storm.
She called out, "Mama Piri"—
she always called her grandmother mama—
who rushed into the room and told her,
"Don't worry . . . it's only your father."

Alberto and Mario, born of different women,
one of whom died giving birth,
stayed in Mexico when Dad left.
By then he had married Mama. She was 11 years younger
and he was almost 40 and still running.
Three more children were born across the border
to become U.S. citizens.
Then a long drive to Watts
where another daughter came.
These were the children he came home to,
the ones who did not get away.
How can I judge?

4.

An Indian-shawled woman trekked across
mountains and desert on an old burro,
just outside the village of Coahuayutla.
In her arms was a baby in weavings,
whimpering in spurts, as the heat
bore down harder with each step
and snakes dangled close to them
from gnarled trees.

Bandits emerged from out of the cactus groves.
"Give us your money, if your life has any value."
The woman pleaded mercy, saying her husband
was with Pancho Villa
and she had to leave because *federales*
were going to raid her town.
"We don't care about no revolution,"
a bandit said. "Nobody cares for us,
but us . . . give us what you got."
She held close the tied wrappings filled with infant.
Another bandit saw the baby and said:
"This is your child, mother?"
"And of a revolutionary," she replied.
"Then go . . . your mother-love
has won you a life."
My grandmother continued on her way;
Dad had crossed his first *frontera*.

5.

Trust was a tree that never stayed rooted;
never to trust a hope of family
never to nurture the branches of a child
awake with ripening fruit.
He trusted less the love we gave
as he mistrusted doctors.
He seldom went to doctors.

One time doctors put him in a hospital
for tests. He had a cough that wouldn't
go away. They had him splayed and tied with tubes
to monitors and plastic bottles.
After a few days, he called my brother and me
to take his car and wait in front of the hospital
steps. When we got there my dad
ran from the front door and into the car.
He had removed all the attachments,
put on his clothes,
sneaked past the nurses station,
and waited by a phone booth for our arrival.
He claimed the hospital was holding
him hostage for the insurance money.
Doctors called and demanded
his return. Dad said never.
He had his own remedies.

6.

He was the one who braved the world's
most heavily guarded border,
the one who sold pots, pans, and insurance,
and worked constructions sites,
the one who endured
the degradations of school administrators,
who refused his credentials,
forced to be a janitor
what they called a "laboratory technician"—
cleaning up animal cages and classrooms;
the closest he would get to a profession.

Every so often, Dad hauled home
hamsters, tarantulas, king snakes,
and fossiled rocks.
My father, the "biologist," named
all the trees and plants
in our yard, gave them stickers

with unpronounceable syllables.
He even named us:
I was *Grillo*—cricket;
my brother became *Rano*, the frog;
Ana was *La Pata*, the duck;
And Gloria, he transformed into *La Cucaracha:*
Cockroach.
By renaming things, he reclaimed them.

7.

All around the room are mounds of papers:
Junk mail, coupons, envelopes (unopened & empty),
much of this sticking out of drawers,
on floor piles—in a shapeless heap
in the corner. On the wooden end
of a bed is a ball made up of thousands
of rubber bands. Cereal boxes
are thrown about everywhere,
some half full. There are writing
tablets piled on one side, filled
with numbers, numbers without pattern,
that you write over and over:
obsessed.

For years your silence
was greeting and departure,
a vocal disengagement.
I see you now walking around in rags,
your eyes glued to Spanish-language *novelas*,
keen to every nuance of voice and movement,
what you rarely gave to me.
This silence is now comfort.

We almost made it, eh Pop?
From the times when you came home late
and gathered up children in both arms
as wide as a gentle wind
to this old guy, visited by police and social workers,
talking to air, accused of lunacy.
I never knew you.
Losing you was all there was.

Cecilia Rodríguez-Milanés

Muchacha (After Jamaica)

Wash your panties and stockings when you take them off; always carry a perfumed handkerchief in your bosom; fry frituritas de bacalao in shimmering hot oil; ask for a little extra when you buy cloth from the polacos; wearing those pointed shoes will cripple you!; don't let me catch you talking to those boys hanging out on a corner by the empty lot; but I don't talk to 'em; you mustn't refer to papaya as papaya but as fruta bomba because people might think you're indecent; it's all right to call those little rolls bollitos though; now that's nasty; this is the way you embroider a woman's hankie; this is the way you embroider a man's; this is the way you mend a sock; this is the way you iron a guayabera without messing up the pleats; this is the way you starch your fine linen blouses that you embroider; this is the way to take la grasa out of the soup; this is the way you sort the frijoles; this is the way you wash the rice; but madrina doesn't wash the rice; plant the cilantro under the kitchen window so you know when it's ready; these are the herbs and spices for the lechoncito, remember to use sour oranges; juice for the mojo on noche buena; this is how you grind the herbs and spices; don't throw the fruta bomba seeds near the house they grow silvestre; this silvestre is used to calm the nerves; this leaf is cut in the middle and spread on burns to prevent scars, it can be drunk too for the lungs but watercress is the best for the lungs; this one is to ease your cramps; this is how you wash the porch; always soak bloodstains in icy cold water; they still won't come out; don't keep any stained clothing; wrap red rags around your fruit trees to ward off the evil eye; always wear your azabache for the same reason, I will give one to your firstborn; never play music on viernes santos; don't ever let me catch you cruis-

178

ing; but you and ...; don't sit with your legs open, it's inde-
cent and you're a decent girl; wash your chocha with that
peach tin can from under the sink, always; don't eat at any-
body's house; don't give your picture to anyone; do not put
your fingers with merengue in the pig's mouth, can't you
see that animal has teeth?; don't dance the merengue too
close; don't let any man stand behind you on the bus; show
your husband everything but your culo, you can never show
a man everything; this is how you make flan; this is how
to despojarte with branches of the paraiso; this is how you
float the gardenias so they don't turn brown, plant them
under the bedroom window when they take root so they
perfume your nights; don't eat all the anones, other people
like them too; this is how you embrace your child; this is
how you embrace someone else's child; I don't have to tell
you how to embrace your husband; this is how you embrace
other women; always saluda when you walk in anywhere,
you're not just anyone, you know; don't wear black bras,
you'll look like the fletera from across the street; always use
the formal usted when speaking to people you don't know;
don't throw dishes at each other when you fight; don't let
your in-laws meddle in your matrimony, that doesn't include
me; don't talk Spanish at the factory/school/office; don't
throw that house out the window; don't drive the oxcart in
front of the oxen; don't make fun of guajiros, your father
will be hurt; don't make fun of gallegos, your grandmother
will be hurt; this is how you take a bath without running
water; this is how to make a cortadito; this is how you save
your pennies; this is how you keep your shoes in good con-
dition; you mustn't let the full moon shine on you when
you're sleeping; when you call someone on the telephone
always say buenos días or buenas tardes, you have manners,
you know; this is how you make camarones enchilados; this
is how you avoid being used, if it happens, it's your own
fault and don't let it happen again; this is where you place
the glasses full of water for the saints; this is where you put
their food; this is how you light a candle for the dead; this
is how you pray for the living; this is how you will mourn

your tierra; but this is my country; this is how you will live in exile; this is how your spirit will rise when your body falls but only after many years, mi hijita, so don't worry about that now.

LEO ROMERO

Again I Find Him

Again I find him
at the bar
drinking a beer
When did I leave you last
I ask him
Last was yesterday
he says
not offering to
buy me a beer
Was it only yesterday
I say
He doesn't say anything
Just into drinking
today
I can see the purple
talk is out of you
I say
He still doesn't say anything
Just looks straight
ahead
with sunglasses on
in this dark bar
The purple talk, I say
that's what you were
talking up
the last time I saw you
He doesn't say anything
to that
Oh, hell, I'll buy
myself a beer
You cheap sona bitch

Mesican, he says
out of the corner
of his mouth
You acting like a Navajo
now, I say to him
Hell, we Pueblos
could kill Mesicans too
he says
Like hell you could
I say
We grow quiet
and brood
Our beers
just a fist away
All that purple talk
talked out of me

Marilyn Monroe Indian

Marilyn Monroe Indian
Luscious cactus
fruit lips
Tight sweater
and tight
black pants
She's got a movie star
look about her
Wind blows up
her dress
and everybody looks
Especially the women
What's she got
that we ain't got
they whisper among
each other

White man approves
of such shapely legs
You're going out
on the town
to Manhattan's
and Los Angeles's
fanciest
You couldn't do
any better
than with
Marilyn Monroe Indian
by your side
Beautiful as she is
she can even read
palms
And no one doubts
her acting abilities
anymore
Me, she says modestly
How could all this
fame
come to me
Little girl
who grew up barefoot
on the reservation
By way of explaining her
other Indians say
She belongs
to the long lost
tribe
of albino Indians
out by Zuni
or someplace

Uncles (Who Lie Still and Perfect)

In memory of my uncles: Guillermo Sáenz, Benjamin Sáenz,
Ricardo Alire, and Bernardo Alire

Guillermo

I would fix my eyes *on him*. He looked right
past me. I was a ghost (as we all were in that slumbering

world of his). Sometimes he suspected I was there:
I wore white shirts, the only color he could see.

Having risen late from a bed he never shared, he sat
stiller than his chair. His waking moments were hard.

He sat solid, immutable, deflecting the light of a sun
that was a heavy burden. He lived for the night, and saw

darkness pasted to his eyes. No stars there, never any
stars. I think he never saw them. The dullness on his

face, a milky film, a veil. Not even the flame of his mother's
anger (nor her impatient love) could peel it from his

skin. At least he knew she was there (and why shouldn't
he know?—He lived with her. She scolded him as she

handed him a second bowl of soup: *Ya basta de tanto trago.*
Te estas matando. Y a mi tambien. Me estas matando. He
   nodded,

almost ashamed. And never answered. His marriage to the
bottle lasted twenty years, a union consummated every
   evening

of his youth. And only after that great divorce that left him
for the first time alone, did he take a wife. He became

a man in mourning, the veil never lifting from his face.
Many years he kept a cancer (something he brought home

from a bar one night—and locked it like a treasure
in his liver). It pounded him month after month, hit him

and hit him until he fell forever in his bed. No liquor
to soften the blows, he fought long as he could. Stranger

that he was, I keep his picture on an altar in my house.
I rise in the morning, his image so familiar I do not

even see it. Now, it is he who's the ghost.

Ricardo

The night
that man
took a brick
to your head
your mother slept.
But there was no
rest for her.
She tossed
and tossed
and she dreamed

        she saw you, happy man

        of her world Your smile

        more real that moment

        than her breath. You sat,

a pebble in your hand, such

joy in simple holdings.

The sun surrounding you

in familiar embrace. She could

see your face, strong, her

peace in you. Your eyes,

the same color as the

cotton leaves of summers

gone, she watched them

close. Then nothing but

clouds. Some large shadow

came between you

and the sun. From where

she slept she cried

"Run!" You could not

see what she saw, could not

hear her voice. All you felt

was the brick

pound your skull.

When the letter arrived

she did not open it.

She had already read

the word that spelled

your death.

My whole life
all I have heard
of you
is that you were
beauty itself.
When your name
is spoken, it is
as if you were
in the room
listening

Bernardo

"*Cada cabeza es un mundo*": the basis of his thought.
The first philosopher I met in the flesh—the only one
I can still quote verbatim. (So much Descartes and Hegel
In the shaping of my mind—and all their words forgotten.
It's true they were smart, true they earned their fame,
Revered and remembered and argued with respectfully—
But what is that to me? What I want to know is
What kind of uncles were they?)

There was something in his step
That made me think he could dance (though I never saw him
Gliding over ball rooms). His walk was dance enough.
The only uncle I ever imagined having sweet and sweaty

187

Sex with his wife of many years. I knew he held her tight
And whispered her name again and again until she was
Safe and asleep. He wasn't ashamed of his mind, of his
Heart, of his penis: the first anti-dualist, anti-oppositional
Thinker in six or seven generations. He never hid his body
From his soul, and at his peak, he argued down ten or twenty
Arm-chair gnostics per night at his favorite bar.

He carried himself like a flame daring the wind to
Blow him out. He never lost his passion for the bottle
Yet he never lost his mind. I yearned to have his fight,
The best of all the graces. *"Mira, mijo, somos
Lo que somos"*: Impossible to live with, he died alone
But did not die unloved. My God, what a heart you had.
What a mind. He left no body of work, no written will,
Not a single letter. What a heart. What a waste.
I've had to settle for reading Plato and Augustine.

Benjamin

On the day of his birth
He took a breath, opened his eyes, then
Closed them tight forever. There was
Something in the Texas air he could never
Be at peace with—too much blood in the dust,
Too much fire in the sun, too much wind,
Too much wind. There would never be enough
Rain. He was born too thirsty. Knowing this
Though he was born perfect and good,
He died.
        Many years passed before his
Surviving older brother (under instructions
From a mother who refused to forget)
Passed down his name to his son.

        This is how I
Came to be possessed of his name, which
In turn, made me fall in love with dead
Uncles who lie still and perfect. Perfect
And good in the ground.

DEBORAH SALAZAR

For Kathy Who Likes Happy Endings

They've never left the second floor apartment
where they were born. You are fascinated
by the tufts of hair that grow
between the pads of their paws.
That's because, I always say,
their feet have never touched the ground.
They tiptoe around on their feathery white footsies,
stretch out on the carpet and lick each other.

Girl-women are so self-conscious and clairvoyant,
with their girl cats, girl intoxicants, girlfriends,
with their feather boas, bulemic purses, boring jobs.
And you, adorable one, have left your mark
—like lipstick on a diet coke can—
at the lacy hem of my loneliness.

I see an old moor tower, way up the purple hill.
And me, waving in the window.
When I throw my hair out that window,
the tresses don't reach the ground.
That's because, I always say,
my hair grows out not down.
So all my curliness unfurls in the sky,
and I float out the window, after my hair.

Alba

We are would-be wives, the both of us.
Nude and smelling like vinyl daisies,

189

we are lying right in front of the house
you will live in when you're married.
Yes, that is an actual cherry pie
on a yellow place-mat on a picnic table.
A tan young man slides under a new car
with a jingly box of tools. Are you awake?—
you ask me, your voice like the hum
of weedeaters, hazy as the sound of pesticides
being sprayed over brilliant green lawns.
We are would-be wives, the both of us.
I kiss your shut eyes, two veined shells
among millions in pieces in the driveway.

For Carrie

Sisters set the table. Each knows her place,
where water glasses, knives, and napkins go.
One loaf bubbles up, a burnt-cheeked face,
while Mama kneads an oily golden dough.
I'm the favorite. The fattest wedge of bread.
Daddy's maraschino cherry gets it all—
the last drop of cola, my sister's head
on a platter. I can't talk; my mouth's full.
She spills salt, burps, smears jam into her peas.
I wash, she dries. Tonight she drops a plate.
She's cut. "Let Mama kiss the bo-bo please."
She shakes her head. That girl deserves her fate.
Never say no to those who love you most.
I know their one rule. I nibble my toast.

You quit speaking in our parents' Spanish,
raised a finger to my lips and hushed me too.
I gave up red meat, made A's in English.
Our mother claims I broke her heart for you.
You grew taller, into our mother's shape,

gave up breakfast, the clarinet, and God.
Mama warned, "Don't be *putas*. All men rape."
You never earned her slow approving nod.
But I could swim faster, fast longer, lose
more marbles than you. See, I suck my thumb.
My dinner's downstairs. *Empanadas* and peas.
"Come down baby," she calls to me. "Please come."
Our men will whisper we're chilly, like silk.
Sister, sister, our skin's made of her milk.

VIRGIL SUAREZ

Izquierdo

The phlegmy coughs resounded and echoed in the lazy afternoon hours when I was home from school. Izquierdo in nothing but shorts and a stained undershirt—who no matter the weather always sat on the sofa of the hostel rooms he and his wife Eloisa and my parents and I shared—was dying of throat cancer, but he wouldn't stop smoking cigarettes and, whenever he wanted to make his wife suffer, cigars, the cheap stinky kind that left an awful stench on all my clothes. He sat on the sofa in silence, smoking and nodding at the plumes of smoke that whirled into his eyes. He continued to smoke, even when the doctor had told him not to do it anymore, even when he knew it was too late to stop because he was dying. But he didn't *want* to stop. "Period," as he would put it. "Punto y aparte!" And Eloisa would leave each time he sat there smoking for she couldn't stand the sight of him killing himself. My parents didn't know it but many an afternoon I would spy on Izquierdo smoking and nodding and sometimes muttering to himself in his native Cuban spanish, once in a while a "coño" becoming audible. All he ever talked about was what he had lost...his homeland...his house...his/his/his. I would spy on him to make sure that he would not be using the bathroom any time soon, since I was twelve and afternoons had become my time to masturbate. This was my secret. The way Izquierdo smoked; I masturbated. Through the bathroom door I would hear him cough, loud grinding and wheezing cough. Izquierdo sat there through the winter, spring, and well into the summer, smoking, smoking, smoking—leaving a trail of ashes and tobacco all over the living room and hallway that ended at the entrance of his and Eloisa's room door. Eloisa once told him that if he saved all the cigarette butts of cigarettes he had consumed, he could fill many buckets. "You've filled your lungs," she said to him one afternoon, "with that poison, and I want no part of it. *Me oyes?*" That was the same afternoon that I went into the bathroom for the last time (I didn't know it would be the last time I would masturbate in the bathroom, that bathroom anyway) and I closed the door. There came a great silence while I put my hands to work. Left first, then right, then both. Those were days of ambidexterity. Suddenly I heard footsteps approach on the other side of the door, then they stopped. Izquierdo, I thought. He tapped on the door and said, "We're going to have to put *cascabeles* around your wrists." Then he walked away. I didn't know what he meant, but I did stop and stood up and raised and buckled my pants and walked out of the bathroom a little embarrassed as if he had been able to see what I was doing through the door. Next time he saw me, which was a couple of days later, he smiled behind a few puffs of smoke, looked at me from across the smoke filled room and said, "Good afternoon, *Cascabeles*." I returned to the room I shared with my parents and sat on the bed confused, for I was beginning to understand what he had meant. *Jingle bells.*

Jicotea/Turtle

They arrived in yute sacks. Their carapaces forming lumps as they pushed against the woven string of the brown sacks. Once my father put down the sack on the cemented patio of the house in Havana, I walked around the lumpy pile intrigued. I was still at an age where guesswork led to endless questions. My father said he'd gotten lucky this time at La Cienega de Zapata, a pocket of the province of Las Villas. My father was from this swampy area of the island of Cuba. *What is it?* I asked. *Jicoteas* he said and smiled, then reached into his shirt pocket for a cigarette. This was the time when my father still smoked even though he suffered from asthma.

Jico—I began but my tongue stumbled over the word—*teaas?*
Tortuguitas, let me show you one. He opened the mouth of
the sack and reached into it the way a magician might into
his hat to pull out a rabbit by the ears. It appeared: a turtle.
Startled, waving its claws? Feet? Legs? In the air as if making
a futile attempt at a swim/escape. *See?* My father asked.
Surely you've been shown pictures at school. (At school we'd
only been shown pictures of Camilo Cienfuegos, Che Gue-
vara, Jose Marti, Karl Marx, Maximo Gomez, Vladimir Lenin,
etc...) *Give me a hand* he said. At first I was reluctant, but
then my father turned the sack upside down and let about
thirty of these turtles free. *But they'll get away,* I told him.
And again, he smiled, then blew smoke out of his nostrils.
No, no, no, he said. *See how they move? They are slow. They
can't get away fast enough.* Get away from what, I thought.
Indeed these *slowpo* creatures tried to make a path on the
cemented patio—and I swear—making little scratch sounds
with their nails against the surface. My father crushed the
cigarette under his shoe, reached to the sheath tied to the
side of his right thigh, and pulled out his sharp machete.
This is what I want you to do, son, he said and showed me.
He grabbed one of the turtles, stepped on it so that it couldn't
move, then with his free hand he pulled and extended the
neck of the turtle. *Like this, see?* He stretched....I looked,
not catching on yet. Then, to my surprise, he swung the
machete downward so fast. There was a loud crushing sound.
There was a spark as the machete sliced through the turtle's
neck and hit the hard concrete underneath. The creature's
neck lay on the floor like a piece of rotted plantain. It was
still twitching as I looked up at my father who was saying,
It's that simple, you grab and pull and I chop. As reluctant
as I was, I did as I was told. I grabbed every one of those
thirty turtles' necks, pulled without looking into their eyes,
and closed my eyes each of the thirty times the machete
came down. Turtle, after turtle, after turtle. All thirty. *After
this you help me clean up, no,* my father was saying. *We
need to remove the shells so that your mother can clean
the meat and cook it.* Yes, we were going to eat these turtles,

these *jicoteas* (the sound of the word now comes naturally) and there was nothing I could say on behalf of the creatures I had helped my father slaughter. And so the idea of death had been inflicted upon me quickly, almost painlessly, with the sacrifice of thirty *jicoteas*.

CARMEN TAFOLLA

Letter to Ti

—From Le Van Minh, 15 and Amerasian, after arriving in the U.S. from Viet Nam, having spent the last four years surviving being fed by and carried on the back of a friend called "Ti."

It is strange being here
like yellow fog wrapped softly around a dream.
The wrapping paper comes undone
and inside I see my face
reflected.
Now, I do not try to look less American.
I should try to look less Vietnamese.
But most times, I just rest,
and don't try anything at all.
The time to close one's eyes is good here
Except that I see you,
the stiff hairs on the back of your neck
laying flatter
with the sweat,
your hard breathing and your bony shoulders
body-friends to my riding body.
As much as I loved your eyes,
the back of your neck was just as dear to me,
the straining neck smiled just as much,
the light shone from around your ears
like the gentle friendship of your face
looking at me.
I knew your neck better than anyone.

Many carry me here.
There will be a chair too
in which I can carry myself.
I eat every meal.

I am in a bed at night.
People do not laugh at me
for my features,
my spine or legs.
I no longer make paper flowers.

I unwrap gifts from people I do not know.
The wrapping paper falls aside.
Sometimes I pick it up and fold it curve it
lay my cheek against it.
"Are you making flowers?" they ask me.
"No.
A neck.
The back of a neck,
Four years my home . . .
and still."

Marked

Never write with pencil,
m'ija.
It is for those
who would
erase.
Make your mark proud
        and open,
Brave,
            beauty folded into
    its imperfection,
Like a piece of turquoise
        marked.

Never write
with pencil,
m'ija.

Write with ink
         or mud,
or berries grown in
gardens never owned,
   or, sometimes,
      if necessary,
         blood.

Compliments

They say I don't look thirty
They also say
I don't look Mexican.
They mean them, I guess,
as compliments.

If that is so,
then it must be
complimentary
to not be
thirty
or
Mexican.

Therefore,
I guess,
they don't
(as much)
like people
who are over
thirty
or too
Mexican.

But now they know
and therefore, I guess
it means
that now
they don't
(as much)
like me.

DAVID UNGER

Night in Oaxaca

for Paul Pines

Wearing *Mixtec* jeans, guaraches, and a shellbead necklace
the Weeping Woman wanders through
the crowded Oaxacan square.
Her gaze, under matted blond hair, is aimless
as if a sorcerer had hexed her.
Her soul flees
through speckled gray eyes,
and she flops down on a bench
under the shadow of a giant moth
clinging to the park light above her.
The marimba music penetrates
the square—balloons bobbing,
armadillo masks laughing, ghosts
crisscrossing her path.
As she drops off to sleep, the moth
turns into a whiskered bat:

her *tona* chews off her rags,
strips her bare—in a dream
under the bandshell, she's back
at Santa Monica Beach,
night wind whistling through a splintering pier,
and a boy who was her friend
pounces. Her body quakes mechanically,
her spooked eyes open.

The Girl in the Treehouse

There once was a girl
who built
a treehouse so high
she could see everything clearly.
And it's true, that from this
    treehouse
she felt the wind blowing
long before the people below,
and she knew when a storm was
    coming.
Once, she even saw the earth
throwing its coat over the moon,
and the moon turned slightly red.
It gave her the kind of power
palmreaders or soothsayers have,
the power a sailor
on the masthead of a sailing ship
must have felt before the world
    had radar.

And she guarded this power
because it was hers alone
and she felt responsible
to warn those below.
It was an awful power
because no one else had it
    and, also,
because she sometimes saw
occurrences she could not stop:
a bird falling out of the sky,
a thunderbolt striking
an unsuspecting snoozer
curled under a tree.
And then there was the fog,
a loam so thick she decided
it was infested with white worms:

no one had warned her,
she hadn't thought to ask
and it pained her to hear screams
or thudding sounds
and not know
from where they had come.

Then she discovered something else:
there was no way,
no way at all,
to communicate with those below.
It made her sad
because seeing
was such an awesome thing,
And so, she came down
from the treehouse in the sky
and resumed her ho-hum life.

This seeing,
which she once confessed to a diver
who plunged into a blue hole
that she never crawled out of again,
the girl did not forget:
it was a gift, a burden
that sometimes made her shudder
at pizza parties or roller rinks,
or when she was surrounded
by so much foolishness
that she thought the treehouse
had been nothing but an empty
   dream.

GINA VALDEZ

English Con Salsa

Welome ESL 100, English Surely Latinized,
ingles con chile y cilantro, English as American
as Benito Juarez. Welcome, muchachos from Zochicalco,
Learn the language of dolares and dolores, of kings
and queens, of Donald Duck and Batman. Holy Toluca!
In four months you'll be speaking like George Washington,
in four weeks you can ask, More coffee? in two months
you can say, may I take your order? in one year you
can ask for a raise, cool as the Tuxpan River.

Welcome, muchachas from Teocaltiche, in this class
we speak English refrito, English con sal y limon,
English thick as mango juice, English poured from
a clay jug, English tuned like a requinto from Uruapan,
        English lighted by Oaxacan dawns,
English spiked
with mezcal from Juchitan, English with a red cactus
flower blooming in its heart.

Welcome, welcome, amigos del sur, bring your Zapotec
tongues, your Nahuatl tones, your patience of pyramids,
your red suns and golden moons, your guardian angels,
your duendes, your patron sainto, Santa Tristeza,
Santa Alegria, Santo Todolopuede. We will sprinkle
holy water on pronouns, make the sign of the cross
on past participles, jump like fish from Lake Patzcuaro
on gerunds, pour tequila from Jalisco on future perfects,
say shoes and shit, grab a cool verb and a pollo loco
and dance on the walls like chapulines.

When a teacher from La Jolla or a cowboy from Santee
asks you, Do you speak English? You'll answer, Si, yes,
simon, of course. I love English!

                                          And you'll hum
a Mextec chant that touches la tierra and the heavens.

Where You From?

Soy de aqui
y soy de alla
from here
and from there
born in L.A.
del otro lado
y de este
creci en L.A.
y en Ensenada
my mouth
still tastes
of naranjas
con chile
soy del sur
y del norte
creci zurda
y norteada
cruzando fron
teras crossing
San Andreas
tartamuda
y mareada
where you from?
soy de aqui
y soy de alla
I didn't build

this border
that halts me
the word fron
tera splits
on my tongue

The Hands

Depending on the light, of the hairy
sun or of the moon, of the shade, of
a tamarind at noon or a chapel at dusk,
the hands, these hands, my hands, your
hands, will appear cream or cinnamon,
pink, red, black or yellow—our heritage.

These are hands of congas, of requintos,
guiros, claves, bongos and timbales, of
maracas, charangos, guitarrones and marimbas,
castanets, tambourines and cymbals, tin tin
timbaleo tingo, these hands sing, dance,
clap to the beat of corn rhumbaing on its way
to becoming a tortilla, these hands round
albondigas and dreams, circle waists, sighs
and hips, peel bananas, masks and mangos,
add, subtract, multiply on blackboards,
beds and griddles, these hands speak fluent
Spanish, they warm, they reduce fevers,
sometimes they write poetry, sometimes
they recite it, these hands could take
away all pain.

These hands, tied by centuries of rope
to ovens, to tables and to diapers, to
brooms, mops, trays and dusters, to saws
and hammers, to picks, hoes and shovels,

they scrub floors, plates and lies, pick
strawberries, grapes, insults and onions,
plant corn, mint, hope and cilantro,
piece by piece they unearth our history.

These hands, so large, so small, two
hummingbirds, quiet, still, joined,
pierced by a nail of U.S. steel, unbind,
shout, close into a fist of sorrow, of
anger, of impatience, these raised hands
open, demand the same as they produce,
as they are giving, these hands smile
in triumph.

GLORIA VANDO

New York City Mira Mira Blues

From the freeway you can almost
hear them screaming in their
red brick coops (no hyphen, please)
HELP ME, HELP ME
through glass grids silhouetted
like chicken wire against the
skyscrapers of Madison, Fifth,
Park, and lately Third Avenue,
where the old el used to shield
the homeless, now homes the shielded.
¡Ay, bendito! What did they do
to this city in their urgent need
to sprinkle liberalism like holy water
on the heads of the oppressors?
They should have played fair, hombre:
they should have left the *jíbaros*
in the mountains of their Isla Bonita,
perched like birds of paradise
on Cerro Maravillas observing
the rise and fall of the earth's curve
as it slumbers beneath the sea;
left them in El Fanguito, squatting
on the squatters squatting on the land
that once was theirs; left them
in Borinquen, where there was no cool
assessment of who owned what,
no color line splitting families
in two or three, where everyone,
todo el mundo, was tinted
with *la mancha de plátano*—but no,
they needed votes. Sure votes.

Had to buy them, fly them in by
planeloads, skies darkening thickly
with visions of barrios to come.
Since it was so easy getting in,
you'd think it would be easy getting out,
but where to go, and who'll take you in?
Take you in, yes; but give you shelter?

The Triborough Bridge, 50 years old
in gold cloth 50 feet high spanning
its towers, waves greetings to us as
we cross the East River, where I swam
as a child, running home as fast as
I could to stash my sopping clothes
in the hamper before Abuelita found
out and exiled me to my island bed.
Now dressed in punk colors, FDR Drive
shouts SAVE EARTH: GIVE A SHIT and
raises a SHAKER-KLASS-AMERICA fist
to the inmates on Welfare Island
whose view ah the view of the
newyorkcityskyline is optimum,
while the Old Rich on tree-lined
Sutton Place only get to see slums.
Welfare Island whose one aesthetic
function is to spew enough smoke
and soot into the air to obscure
Queens and itself, if the wind
is right, in a merciful eclipse.
Welfare Island, where our poet
Julia de Burgos was confined, forgotten,
all her protest silenced with yet
another 2 c.c.'s of thorazine.

On 110th Street, my concrete manger
overlooking Central Park, only Spanish
signs remain to remind us of the second-
to-the-last immigration wave: Cubanos

seeking refuge when class status takes
a backseat to red slogans, red tape.
The Bay of Pigs non-invasion spurs
them on to invade us, Miami first, then
slowly up the coast like a spreading
thrombosis that ruptures in Nueva York,
where all Hispanics blend into one
faceless thug, one nameless spic.

The cab cuts like a switchblade
across the park; I try to hear Ives'
marching bands meeting in noisy combat
on Sheep Meadow, but later sounds
intrude, reintroduce themselves
like forgotten kin—midnight, a baby
carriage, my mother crossing the park
from her sitter's on the eastside
to her husband's on the west. And she,
loving the leaves' black dance against
the night, recalls her mother's warning
that she not try to blot out the sky
with one hand, but oh! there beneath
the trees, the immensity of space is
palpable—she feels safe. And lacing
the earth, a fragrance she cannot discern
causes her to yearn for home. She hums

half expecting the coquis to sing along.
It is that time of night when muggers
are out—even then before the word
was out—blending into shadows, bushes,
trees, like preview footage of Vietnam,
waiting to assault whatever moves,
whatever breathes. She breathes hard

but moves so fast they cannot keep up.
West Side Story before they learned
that death set to music could make
a killing at the boxoffice. With one
Robbins-like leap up a steep incline
we escape; I sleep through it. Now
I'm wide awake watching every leaf quake
in the wind as her young limbs in flight
must have then, fifty years ago
on that moonless night in Central Park
where fifty years before that
sheep grazed and innocence prevailed.

We exit on 86th Street, head down
Central Park West, past the Dakota
to our safe harbor in the heart
of Culture and Good Manners with
Lincoln Center only steps away.
Next door a flop house. Old people
with swollen legs sunning themselves
on folding chairs, used shopping
bags with someone's trash,
their treasure, at their feet.
The buzzards of the human race
cleaning up other people's droppings.
We walk around them, as though
proximity could contaminate. Nearby
those less prosperous prop themselves
up against their own destruction.
I see my children stepping carefully
between them, handing out coins
like Henry Ford. I see them losing
faith, losing hope, losing ground.
But I am home, *home,* I tell myself.
Home from the wheat and the corn
of Middle America, where whole-
someness grows so tall you cannot
see the poverty around you, grows

so dense the hunger cannot touch you.
Home to the familiar, the past; my
high school moved comfortably closer,
renamed LaGuardia for the Little Flower
who captured our hearts with
Pow! Wham! and *Shazam!* on newsless
Sunday mornings during the war.
Home to my Westside condo with free
delivery from columns A to Z,
a xenophobic's dream come true.
Home to the city's long shadows
casting tiers up, across, and down
skyless streets and buildings,
an Escher paradox turning a simple
journey to the corner into a fantasy
in chiaroscuro. Yes, I'm home,
home, where my grandmother's aura
settles softly and white like
a shroud of down, stilling, if only
for a moment, the island's screams.

Cante Jondo

Segovia says Lorca was killed
by a jealous lover, but I know
that isn't so, I know he was seized
from midnight reverie, pried screaming
from the poem in his head, the lover
beside him pleading with Franco's men
before the butt end of a German carbine
careened him into a wordless sleep
taking him worlds away from Lorca
Guernica, and the caves of Andalucia
from the fifth column, the Flange, death—
far, far from death, deep into a dream

sweetened by seas, seeping slowly
into Moroccan fields where boys
culipandeando ignite the lighteyed
lust of tourists who come down
to excavate their scraggly yield—
Arabs preferring the ripe, moist meat
of melons—and Lorca's lover lying
in that crazy hard-on dream, oblivious
of what was going on, unconscious
of his own demise—with the poet gone
who would immortalize his soul?—and
the barrel of a rifle prodding Lorca's
chest like the insistent finger of Uncle
Sam, hard up against his anus, prying
open his mouth *muévelo, maricón* and
Lorca's face green as the craters
of his vellum moon, his body twisted,
a hibiscus against the dawn, stumbles
ahhh! as they jab him on, blindfold
filth across his eyes, *those eyes,* bind
laces from his shoes into his wrists so
when he staggers to the wall his shoes
drag through the gravel, unravelling
the earth's tears, the earth's dark song

      drrrggge drrrggge dirige *Domine*
      Deus meus in conspectu tuo viam meam

Lorca, my poet, shot down the prayer
while his lover unaware sleeps and dreams
of almond eyes and bougainvillea.
Homosexuals die violent deaths, Segovia
says, playing a Bach fugue on his guitar.

Ronda

On Tuesday they moved her father's
body from the temporary grave granted
it by the state to a private plot
on the outskirts of San Juan. "Not

too far away," her sister assures her.
"When you come this summer we'll
visit. I think you'll like it better."
Her stepmother spent the year

making coquito out of coconut
milk and rum. She sold enough bottles
at Christmas to raise the $350 it cost
to move her father's body across

town. She marvels at her zeal,
but thinks, too, of his impending ordeal,
of his bones having to make fresh
indentations in the soil, his flesh

having to warm the land around him.
Even in death he seems condemned
to suffer life's transgressions—
forced to break in a final mattress,

to take in a final mistress.

E. J. VEGA

Why My Mother's Teeth Remained in Cuba

The great Don, Pepe Jartin, carried
His middle daughter downhill
Writhing in pain to the dentist
(Who was also the village blacksmith).
"Saving the tooth will cost two pesos,"
Said the dentist while shaping hot steel
Rods into horseshoes. "To extract, one."
The great Don readjusted the brim
Of his fedora, gazed up at the mountains
Of his daughter's birth, and at his 30,000
Acres of coffee beans that, at times, tumbled
To the earth like bright gumdrops. Raising
One finger to heaven, he faced the dentist
Who wiped burn-scarred hands on a leather
Apron and strapped the girl to an armchair.

First Breakfast

What else if not pennybread,
And coffee
After the ferry's bolted
Like a whipped ox
Back to Ellis Island?

Cringing at the sound
Of planks protesting
The recent abuse,
You spill the coffee

And flag the waitress
For a 2nd cup
(No tan lleno, por favor).

On leaving you till
Your pockets for change
And yield the crop
Of twenty years' saving as tip.

For now, Liberty
Comes like your coffee:
Black No Sugar.

Delicious Death

to my son, Marc

Memory: You were fifteen in the mountains,
your friends were going hunting,
you wanted to go.

Cold, autumn day-sky of steel
and rifles, the shade of bullets. We
fought. I didn't want to let you go.

And you stood up to me, "My friends are
going, their parents let them hunt, like
am I some kind of wimp or what, Mom..."

We walked into Thrifty's to buy the bullets,
you would use one of their rifles—I imagined
you being shot or shooting another eager boy/man.

"What you kill you eat, do you understand?"
I stared each word into your eyes. As you
walked away, I said to the Spirits, "Guard

this human who goes
in search of
lives."

*   *   *   *

You brought home four small quail.
I took them saying, "Dinner." I stuffed
them with rice, apples, baked them in garlic,

onions, wine. "Tonight, Mom?" "Yes, tonight."
I plucked the softest tail feathers and as you
showered, I placed them in your pillow case:

"May the thunder and
the prey be
one.

May the hunter eat
and be eaten in
time.

May the boy always
be alive in the
man."

       *   *   *   *

We ate, mostly, in silence—
I felt you thinking, I just
killed this, what I'm chewing . . .

On the highest peaks the first
powder shines like the moon—
winter comes so quickly.

On your face soft, blonde hair (yes, this
son is a gringo) shines like manhood—
childhood leaves so quickly.

The wonder of the hunt is on my tongue,
I taste it—wild, tangy, reluctant—
this flesh feeds me well.

I light the candles and thank the quail
in a clear voice—I thank them for their
small bodies, their immense, winged souls.

217

"God, Mom, you're making me feel like a
killer." "Well, you are and so am I."
Swallowing, swallowing this delicious death.

The Wind

I wanted to be your friend
        (the mountains roared like
        Vietnam, you said)—

I wanted to be your lover
        (the lightning kept me up
        with wonder, staring)—

I wanted to accept the light
        (the rain was soft and chill,
        I made us tea, laughing)—

I wanted to accept the darkness
        (the trail is dry and stony,
        makes us sweat, trip, curse)—

I cannot translate the language of
the mountains, or give you light,
or take your darkness, or ease
your memories, or make you wonder—

I can only want.
The rest is up
to you. My wanting
is the wind—invisible

and real. It clings
to nothing, changes everything

in its path in some small way.
I want the wind.

The Sierras in August—

An Act of Creation

to Cesar Chavez

They keep rounding them up
through the centuries, killing
the innocent, so easily—

the babies, the children,
the screaming mothers—
the men who do not beg

for mercy. Yes, yes, they
keep rounding up the victims,
again and again—their only

heirloom, possession: poverty.
When I was a young mother, I
didn't fully realize this—
in my stupidity, I thought

the children were spared.

And when I thought of wolves
and lambs, I thought of
one or the other. A wolf.
A lamb. One bloodthirsty, eating
raw, red meat. One gentle, nibbling

grass. Now, twenty years later, they
still round up the innocent, or

corral them (as in South Africa),
slowly starving their flesh and
spirit to death. The enemy

kills the enemy's children.

A stubborn man fasts for
the farmworkers—their children
are not born whole, and ours
will not be born whole. That

is an act of creation.

Like painting a mural, a
watercolor, like composing
a symphony, like writing
a story, a poem.

That is when the lamb
and the wolf lie down,
together, and make extraordinary,
exquisite, ecstatic. Love.

Until the next round-up.

Or until we learn better—
that without the lamb, the
wolf starves, and without the
wolf, the lamb grows fat
and stupid. Yes, I understand

why the stubborn man
does not eat, pretending
to be a lamb, inviting
the wolves to feast
upon his sweet, brown

flesh. His spirit.

TINO VILLANUEVA

Scene from the Movie *GIANT*

What I have from 1956 is one instant at the Holiday
Theater, where a small dimension of a film, as in
A dream, became the feature of the whole. It
Comes toward the end . . . the café scene, which
Reels off a slow spread of light, a stark desire

To see itself once more, though there is, at times,
No joy in old time movies. It begins with the
Jingling of bells and the plainer truth of it:
That the front door to a roadside café opens and
Shuts as the Benedicts (Rock Hudson and Elizabeth

Taylor), their daughter Luz, and daughter-in-law
Juana and grandson Jordy, pass through it not
Unobserved. Nothing sweeps up into an actual act
Of kindness into the eyes of Sarge, who owns this
Joint and has it out for dark-eyed Juana, weary

Of too much longing that comes with rejection.
Juana, from barely inside the door, and Sarge,
Stout and unpleased from behind his counter, clash
Eye-to-eye, as time stands like heat. Silence is
Everywhere, acquiring the name of hatred and Juana

Cannot bear the dread—the dark-jowl gaze of Sarge
Against her skin. Suddenly: bells go off again.
By the quiet effort of walking, three Mexican-
Types step in, whom Sarge refuses to serve . . .
Those gestures of his, those looks that could kill

221

A heart you carry in memory for years. A scene from
The past has caught me in the act of living: even
To myself I cannot say except with worried phrases
Upon a paper, how I withstood arrogance in a gruff
Voice coming with the deep-dyed colors of the screen;

How in the beginning I experienced almost nothing to
Say and now wonder if I can ever live enough to tell
The after-tale. I remember this and I remember myself
Locked into a back-row seat—I am a thin, flickering,
Helpless light, local-looking, unthought of at fourteen.

Haciendo Apenas La Recolección

For weeks now
I have not been able
to liberate me from my name.
Always I am history I must wake to.
In idiot defeat I trace my routes
across a half-forgotten map of Texas.
I smooth out the folds stubborn
as the memory.

Let me see: I would start from San Marcos,
moving northward,
bored beyond recognition
in the stale air of a '52 Chevy:
to my left, the youngest of uncles
steadies the car;
to my right, grandfather finds humor
in the same joke.
I am hauled among family
extended across the back seat,
as the towns bury themselves forever
in my eyes: Austin, Lampasas, Brownwood,

past Abilene, Sweetwater,
along
the Panhandle's alien tallness.
There it is: Lubbock sounding harsh as ever.
I press its dark letters,
and dust on my fingertips is so alive
it startles them
as once did sand.
Then west, 10,000 acres and a finger's breadth,
is Levelland
where the thin house once stood,
keeping watch over me and my baseball glove
when the wrath of winds cleared the earth
of stooping folk.
There's Ropesville, where in fifth grade
I didn't make a friend.

My arm is taut by now and terrified.
It slackens,
begins falling back to place,
while the years are gathering slowly
along still roads and hill country,
downward
to where it all began—500 McKie Street.
I am home, and although the stars
are at rest tonight,
my strength is flowing.

Weep no more, my common hands;
you shall not again
pick cotton.

March 1979–January 1980

RAFAEL ZEPEDA

Pony

When I first met Pony he wouldn't
touch a drink. He dealt pot and
he worked at an aircraft factory
and had a blonde girl friend
who he said was crazy.

He let me stay at his place
overlooking the Pacific.
He bought me canvas to paint on,
gave me food to eat.
He kept me alive.

Now Pony calls me from bars
where loud music is playing
in the background.
He says, "Ray, what's happening
man. How's the lady, the kid,
how's the writing, you're a painter,
how's the painting? Man, I'd like
to see you, but you know how it is.
Having a good time and living
the life. Maybe I've got a gig
going."

A year later he calls.
"Ray, what's happening man?
How's the . . .
How's the . . .
"What ever happened to that lady
you were with?" I ask him.

"Where have you been?"
"At the end of the earth, man."
"Where are you now?"
"Man," he says, "don't ask metaphysical
questions."

Trans Pacific

We were in the middle of the Pacific
on a liberty ship.
We'd dumped some bombs off in Guam.
They were going to Vietnam.
The 2nd electrician was a Mexican
called Ernie who'd told me that once
when he'd signed off a ship in Galveston
he'd taken 3 thousand dollars to a madam
at a local whorehouse, and he'd stayed there
for a month He'd never even gone out the door.
"The best month of my life," he said.
I liked him.
But there was an oiler from Arizona
who seemed like a good guy
and we stood on the fan tail and talked,
one afternoon. Nothing around us but ocean.
The generator of the ship kept breaking down
and had been doing it for months.
"It's that damned Mexican, the 2nd electrician," the oiler
     said.
"I got a ranch down in Arizona
and once in a while these wetbacks come through
so I give them a job, for room and board.
Next thing you know they're wanting money
and waiting to leave . . . I don't know what
it is, but those Mexicans are just born
lazy, I guess."

"That's funny," I said. "My father's a Mexican
and he ain't lazy."
That was the end of the conversation.
He was on the ship for another two months
but I never saw him again.
I guess he thought that I was coming
in the night to stick him with my push button.
He didn't know that I'd lost it, when I was 10.
Ernie paid off in Panama.
There was a whorehouse that he liked there
called the Blue Goose.

Biographical Notes

JULIA ALVAREZ was born in the Dominican Republic and emigrated to the United States in 1960. She published her first collection of poems, *Homecoming*, in 1984. A novel, *How the Garcia Girls Lost Their Accents* (Algonquin), was the winner of the 1991 PEN-Oakland/Josephine Miles Book Award. Alvarez is currently professor of English at Middlebury College and is working on a new novel.

JIMMY SANTIAGO BACA was born in Santa Fe, New Mexico. He is the author of the following collections of poetry: *Immigrants in Our Own Land*, *Black Mesa Poems*, and *Martin & Meditations on the South Valley* (New Directions), for which he won the 1988 Before Columbus American Book Award. Most recently he has published a book of nonfiction entitled *Working in the Dark: Reflections of a Poet of the Barrio*. His movie, *Bound By Honor*, was a popular as well as a critical success. Mr. Baca lives with his family on a small farm outside Albuquerque, New Mexico.

SANDRA M. CASTILLO has published poems in many magazines, including the *Apalachee Quarterly*, *Florida Review*, and *Polyphony*. Her first book, *Red Letters*, was published by Apalachee Press. She lives in Miami, Florida.

ADRIAN CASTRO was born in 1967 in Miami, and is of Cuban and Dominican heritage. He writes in the rhythmic Afro-Cuban/Caribbean tradition pioneered by Nicolàs Guillén and Luis Pales Matos. He has performed his poetry nationwide, in solo as well as with his percussion poetry band, Burning Tongues. His poems have been published in *Bilingual Press Review*, *The Miami Herald*, *Bombay Gin*, *The New Censorship*, and in periodicals in Mexico. He is currently translating selected works of Luis Pales Matos.

ROSEMARY CATACALOS is the author of a hand letterpress chapbook, *As Long as It Takes* (Iguana Press, St. Louis, 1984) and a full-length collection, *Again for the First Time* (Tooth of Time Books, Santa Fe, 1984) which received the Texas Institute of Letters Poetry Prize in 1985. She is presently Executive Director of The Poetry Center/American Poetry Archives at San Francisco State University, where she also teaches creative writing.

LORNA DEE CERVANTES is the author of *Emplumada* (University of Pittsburgh Press, 1981) and *From the Cables of Genocide: Poems of Love and Hunger* (Arte Publico Press, 1991), which was awarded the Paterson Poetry Prize in 1992. Cervantes teaches creative writing at the University of Colorado, Boulder.

JUDITH ORTIZ COFER was born in Hormigueros, Puerto Rico and grew up in Paterson, New Jersey. She is the author of *Terms of Survival* (Arte Publico Press), a memoir; *The Line of The Sun* (University of Georgia Press), a novel; and a collection of prose and poetry, *The Latin Deli* (University of Georgia Press). Cofer travels extensively, giving readings and lectures. She lives in Georgia.

LUCHA CORPI was born in the state of Veracruz, Mexico. She is the author of two collections of poetry in Spanish, translated by Catherine Rodríguez-Nieto, *Palabras de Mediodia/Noon Words* (Fuego de Aztlán Publications, 1980), *Variaciones sobre una tempestad/Variations on a Storm* (Third Woman Press, 1990); and of two novels, *Delia's Song* and *Eulogy for a Brown Angel* (Arte Publico Press, 1989 and 1992). *Eulogy for a Brown Angel* won the PEN-Oakland/Josephine Miles Literary Prize. Corpi is a founding member and former president of Aztlán Cultural/Centro Chicano de Escritores (Chicano Center for Writers). She is also a teacher in the Oakland Public Schools' Neighborhood Centers Program.

VICTOR HERNÁNDEZ CRUZ was born in Aguas Buenas, Puerto Rico. In New York City in the mid-1960s he started writing and publishing. His poems appeared in *Evergreen Review, The Village Voice,* and *Ramparts.* He is the author of *Snaps* (Random House, 1969), *Mainland* (Random House, 1973), and *Red Beans* (Coffee House Press, 1991). In the mid-1970s Victor Hernández Cruz moved to the San Francisco Bay area, where he lived for many years before returning to Puerto Rico in 1989. He now lives in Aguas Buenas, and is working on a novel, as well as on his first book of poems written directly in Spanish.

SILVIA CURBELO was born in Matanzas, Cuba, in 1955 and emigrated to the U.S. in 1967. She was co-winner of the 1992 James Wright Poetry Award from *Mid-American Review,* and is the author of a collection of poetry, *The Geography of Leaving* (Silverfish Review Press). Curbelo is also poetry and fiction editor for *Organica Quarterly,* in Tampa.

MARTÍN ESPADA is the author of four volumes of poetry: *The Immigrant Iceboy's Bolero* (1982); *Trumpets from the Islands of Their Eviction* (1987); *Rebellion Is the Circle of a Lover's Hands* (Curbstone, 1990), winner of the Paterson Poetry Prize; and *City of*

Coughing and Dead Radiators (W. W. Norton, 1993). His work has also appeared in such publications as the *Christian Science Monitor*, *The Kenyon Review*, and *Ploughshares*. Espada works as a tenant lawyer and supervisor of Su Clinica Legal, a legal services program of Suffolk University Law School in Boston.

SANDRA MARIA ESTEVES was born, grew up, and still lives in the Bronx. She is of Puerto Rican and Dominican heritage. Esteves has published three volumes of poetry: *Bluestown Mockingbird Mambo*; *Tropical Rains: A Bilingual Downpour*; and *Yerba Buena*, which was a Best of the Small Press publication, awarded by *Library Journal* in 1981.

GUSTAVO PÉREZ FIRMAT was born in Cuba and grew up in Miami, Florida. Currently he is professor of Spanish at Duke University. In addition to several books of literary criticism, he has published three collections of poetry, *Carolina Cuban* (1987), *Equivocaciones* (1989), and *Bilingual Blues* (1994). Firmat lives in Chapel Hill, North Carolina, with his wife and two children.

DIANA GARCIA is from Merced, California, in the San Joaquin Valley. Her grandmothers were from Mexico, her grandfathers from Arizona. She now lives in San Diego, where she teaches at San Diego State University and works part-time as a bilingual consultant in criminal defense work. Garcia's poems have appeared in *Mid-American Review*, *The Haight-Ashbury Literary Journal*, and *The Kenyon Review*. A short story was included in the anthology *Pieces of the Heart* (ed. G. Soto, Chronicle Books).

GUY GARCIA was born in Los Angeles. A contributor to *Time* magazine since 1980, his writing has also appeared in *The New York Times*, *Rolling Stone*, *Interview*, *Premiere*, and *Elle*. His fiction is featured in the anthologies *Iguana Dreams: New Latino Fiction* (ed. V. Suarez, HarperCollins) and *Pieces of the Heart: New Chicano Fiction* (ed. G. Soto, Chronicle Books). He is the author of two novels, including *Obsidian Sky* (Simon & Schuster, 1994). Garcia lives in New York City.

LOURDES GIL was born in Havana and has lived in the United States since 1961. She has worked as a translator for Hearst Publications in New York and has been the recipient of several awards, among them the Cintas Fellowship in 1979. Her poetry and essays have been published in numerous literary magazines. She is the author of *Neumas* (1977), *Manuscrito de la Niña Ausente* (1979), *Vencido el Fuego de la Especie* (1983), and *Blanca Aldaba Preludia* (1989). She is presently co-editor of the literary journal *Lyra*.

MAGDALENA GÓMEZ, poet, playwright, journalist, and performance artist, has shared her work in public readings since 1979. The most recent of her seventeen produced theater works, *In Loving Memory* (written in collaboration with Paul Manship), premiered at the Chicago Palmer Hilton in 1993 for the Parliament of the World's Religions. Gómez is an Artist-in-Residence at the Holyoke Magnet Middle School for the Arts and a company member of the Enchanted Circle Theater, Holyoke, Massachusetts.

RAY GONZALEZ has edited fourteen anthologies, including *Without Discovery: A Native Response to Columbus* (Broken Moon Press); *After Aztlan: Latino Poets in the Nineties* (David R. Godine); and *Currents from the Dancing River: Contemporary Latino Fiction, Nonfiction, and Poetry* (Harcourt Brace). His third book of poetry, *The Heat of Arrivals*, and a collection of essays, *Memory Fever: A Journey Beyond El Paso del Norte*, are published by Broken Moon Press. In 1993 he received a Before Columbus American Book Award for Excellence in Editing. He lives in San Antonio.

CÉSAR A. GONZÁLEZ-T., a Chicano poet and short story writer, was born in South Central Los Angeles. His parents entered the U.S. at the Port of San Pedro, California, from Colima, Mexico, in 1928, refugees of the Cristiada. González-T. was once himself an undocumented worker in Mexico. He now lives in San Diego, and is the founding chair of Chicano Studies at Mesa College. In addition to his fiction and poetry, he is the author of a book of criticism, *Unwinding the Silence and Rudolfo A. Anaya: Focus on Criticism.*

DANIEL DEL VALLE HERNÁNDEZ was born in New York in 1950. He has published two books in Spanish, *Itinerario para emboscar laberintos* and *Fragmentos del otro lado del paraiso.* He is a participant in the Surrealist Movement in the United States and abroad.

JUAN FELIPE HERRERA is the author of many books of poetry, including *Rebozos of Love* (Tolteca Publications), *Exiles of Desire* (Arte Publico Press), *Facegames* (Dragon Cloud Press), *Akrílica* (Alcatraz Editions), *Indian Journey* (Broken Moon Press, 1994) and *New and Selected Poems* (Broken Moon Press, 1995). *Facegames* received the Before Columbus American Book Award. Herrera teaches culture studies, Chicano Teatro, and creative writing at California State University, Fresno.

CAROLINA HOSPITAL is a Cuban American poet, fiction writer, and essayist. Her work has appeared in numerous national magazines, newspapers, and anthologies. She also lectures on the literature of Latinos in the U. S. She is the editor of an anthology, *Cuban American Writers: Los Attrevidos* (Linden Lane Press, 1989), to which she also contributed prose and poetry, and *Everyone Will Have to Listen* (Linden Lane Press, 1990), a bilingual edition of poetry by Tania Diaz Castro, translated by Hospital with Pablo Medina.

WASABI KANASTOGA was born in Cuba and grew up in Los Angeles. He is not a practicing Buddhist and frequently eats red meat. He belongs to no social clubs, organizations, or literary entities. His work seldom appears in print, but he continues to write short stories and poetry nonetheless. Right now he is stuck in Los Angeles freeway traffic; he is hungry and tired and longs to return home to his wife and children.

E. A. MARES teaches creative writing and history at the University of North Texas. His poetry, essays, translations, and works of historical scholarship have appeared in various publications, and his plays have been performed in New Mexico and elsewhere. His most recent book is *The Unicorn Poem & Flower and Songs of Sorrow* (West End Press, 1992), a collection of poems. He has also published *I Returned and Saw Under the Sun* (University of New Mexico Press, 1989), the first published version of his one-man performance based on Padre Antonio José Martínez of Taos, and *Padre Martínez: New Perspectives From Taos* (The Millicent Rogers Museum, 1989), a collection of scholarly essays.

DEMETRIA MARTÍNEZ was born in Albuquerque, New Mexico, in 1960. In 1982 she received her B.A. from the Woodrow Wilson School of Public and International Affairs at Princeton University, where she was a Wilson Scholar. While at Princeton she studied poetry, and has published poems in many anthologies, including *After Aztlan: Latino Poets of the Nineties* (ed. R. Gonzalez, David R. Godine). She is also the author of a novel, *Mother Tongue* (Bilingual Review Press, 1994), and national news editor of the *National Catholic Reporter*, Kansas City, Missouri.

DIONISIO D. MARTÍNEZ was born in Cuba. His book *History as a Second Language* won the 1992 Ohio State University Press/*The Journal* Award in Poetry. *Dancing at the Chelsea* won the 1991 State Street Press Chapbook Competition. He lives in Tampa, Florida, and works in the Poets-in-the-Schools program. He is also public relations consultant for *Organica Quarterly*.

VICTOR MARTÍNEZ is the author of *Caring for a House* (Chusma House Publications). An accomplished short-story writer, Martínez has also written a novel, entitled *Parrot in the Oven*. Presently he is working on a collection of essays on Chicano/Latino artists and poets. Martínez lives and works in San Francisco.

JULIO MARZÁN is the author of *Translations Without Originals* (I. Reed Books, 1986), poetry; and the editor-translator of *Inventing a Word: An Anthology of Twentieth-Century Puerto Rican Poetry* (Columbia University Press, 1980). He has also written a book of criticism, *Foreign Heart: The Spanish American Roots of Williams Carlos Williams* (University of Texas Press, 1994).

PABLO MEDINA was born in Havana, Cuba, and has lived in the United States since 1960. He has published two collections of poems, *Pork Rinds and Cuban Songs* (Nuclassics and Science, 1975) and *Arching Into the Afterlife* (Bilingual Press, 1991), and a novel, *The Marks of Birth* (Farrar, Straus, and Giroux, 1994). He is now on the faculty of the Writing Program at Warren Wilson College. He lives in Miami, Florida.

JESÚS PAPOLETO MELÉNDEZ was born in el barrio, New York City. His books of poetry include *Street Poetry & Other Poems*, *Have You Seen Liberation*, and *Casting Long Shadows*. Meléndez lives and writes on the border between the U. S. and Mexico.

PAT MORA is the author of numerous collections of poetry, including *Agua Santa/Holy Water*, *Chants*, *Borders*, and *Communion* (Arte Público Press); a collection of essays, *Nepantla: Essays from the Land in the Middle* (University of New Mexico Press, 1993); and a children's book, *A Birthday Basket for Tía* (Macmillan, 1992). Originally from El Paso, Texas, Mora now lives in Cincinnati.

GEAN MORENO was born in New York in 1972. From age four to age twelve he lived in Colombia, his father's birthplace. His poems have been published in *Midwest Quarterly* and *Poetry Forum*. Presently he lives in Miami, where he attends Florida International University.

ELÍAS MIGUEL MUÑOZ is a widely published Cuban American poet, novelist, and literary critic. His works include two books of literary criticism and the highly regarded novels *Crazy Love* and *The Greatest Performance*, as well as two collections of poetry, *En Estas Tierras/In This Land* and *No Fue Posible el Sol*. He has contributed to several anthologies of U.S. Latino literature and he has recently completed his fourth novel.

RICARDO PAU-LLOSA, poet, short story writer, and art critic, was born in Havana in 1954 and has lived in the U. S. since 1960. He teaches in the English Department of Miami-Dade Community College. In 1983, Pau-Llosa's book, *Sorting Metaphors*, won the national competition for the first Anhinga Poetry Prize. He has also published *Bread of the Imagined* (Bilingual Press, 1992) and *Cuba*

(Carnegie-Mellon, 1993). As an art critic and curator, Pau-Llosa specializes in twentieth-century Latin American art.

PEDRO PIETRI was born in Ponce, Puerto Rico, and grew up in New York City. He started writing in the 1950s under the influence of Doo-Wop, especially the group Frankie Lymon and the Teenagers. Pietri has had numerous plays produced, and many have been collected in *Illusion of a Revolving Door* (Editorial de la Universidad de Puerto Rico). He is the author of *Puerto Rican Obituary* and *Traffic Violations*, books of poetry; and a short story collection, *Lost in the Museum of Natural History*.

NAOMI QUIÑONEZ was born and grew up in Los Angeles. She is the author of a volume of poems, *Hummingbird Dream*, and the editor of the anthology *Invocation L.A.*, which won a 1990 American Book Award. Quiñonez is widely published in anthologies and literary journals, and has given reading in cities nationwide. Currently she is pursuing a doctorate in American Studies at Claremont Graduate School, where she specializes in the study of women writers of color in the United States.

LEROY V. QUINTANA is a native New Mexican. His books include *Hijo del Pueblo: New Mexico Poems* (New Mexico State University), *Sangre* (Prima Agua Press). *Five Poets of Aztlan* (Bilingual Press), *Interrogations* (Vietnam Generation/Burning Cities Press), and *The History of Home* (Bilingual Press). He has won many awards, including a Border Regional Library Association Award and an American Book Award, both in 1982. Quintana is on the English faculty at Mesa College, San Diego.

ALBERTO ALVARO RÍOS is the author of *Teodoro Luna's Two Kisses, The Lime Orchard Woman, The Warrington Poems, Five Indiscretions, The Iguana Killer,* and *Whispering to Fool the Wind.* His honors include the 1991 Governor's Arts Award, the Walt Whitman Award, the Western States Book Award for Fiction, four Pushcart Prizes, and inclusion in *The Norton Anthology of Modern Poetry.* He is professor of English and Director of the Creative Writing Program at Arizona State University.

DIANA RIVERA writes poetry, short stories, and essays. She is the author of a book of poems, *Bird Language* (Bilingual Review Press). Rivera is also a painter, whose work is exhibited regularly in the United States and in Puerto Rico. She lives in Upper Grandview, New York, on the outskirts of New York City.

MARGARITA LUNA ROBLES is a poet/writer/performance artist. Her published work includes *Triptych: Dreams, Lust and Other*

233

Performances and *A Night in Tunisia* (co-authored with Juan Felipe Herrera). Her poetry, fiction, essays, and reviews have appeared in journals throughout the Southwest. She teaches Chicano Studies at California State University, Fresno.

LUIS J. RODRÍGUEZ is a poet and writer whose articles and reviews have appeared in *The Los Angeles Times, The Nation, Playboy, The Chicago Reporter,* and elsewhere. His first book, *Poems Across the Pavement* (Tia Chucha Press), won a 1989 Book Award from the Poetry Center, San Francisco State University. His second, *The Concrete River* (Curbstone Press), won a 1991 PEN-Oakland/ Josephine Miles Literary Award. His latest book is *Always Running: La Vida Loca, Gang Days in L.A.* (Curbstone Press, 1993), an autobiographical account of growing up in Watts and the East L.A. area.

CECILIA RODRÍGUEZ-MILANÉS was born in New Jersey to Cuban parents. She writes poetry and fiction and teaches writing and multicultural literature at Indiana University of Pennsylvania. She is interested in issues of race, class, ethnicity and gender, not necessarily in that order.

CATHERINE RODRÍGUEZ-NIETO, translator of Lucha Corpi's poetry included here, was born in Minot, North Dakota. She has translated two bilingual volumes of poetry, *Fireflight: Three Latin American Poets* and *Palabras de mediodía/Noon Words: Poems by Lucha Corpi.* She and her husband live in Oakland, California, where they own and operate In Other Words, Inc., a translation and editing service.

LEO ROMERO has published three books of poetry, *Going Home Away Indian, Celso,* and *Agua Negra,* and a collection of stories, *Rita and Los Angeles* (Bilingual Review Press). He owns and works in Books & More Books, a bookstore in Santa Fe, New Mexico.

BENJAMIN ALIRE SÁENZ was born and grew up in Las Cruces, New Mexico. After studying theology in undergraduate and graduate school, he turned to writing. Among his honors are a Wallace Stegner Fellowship in Creative Writing and a 1992 Before Columbus American Book Award for his poetry collection *Calendar of Dust* (Broken Moon Press). He has also published a collection of stories, *Flowers for the Broken* (Broken Moon Press, 1993), and a second collection of poetry, *Dark and Perfect Angels* (Broken Moon Press). He is currently at work on a novel entitled *Carry Me Like Water.*

DEBORAH SALAZAR was born in Guayaquil, Ecuador, but lived most of her life as an illegal alien in the United States. In 1988, she received her MFA in English from Louisiana State University and was granted permanent U.S. residency. Her poems, essays, stories, and translations have appeared in various magazines, textbooks, and anthologies. She has taught at the Naropa Institute in Boulder, Colorado. She lives in Baton Rouge, Louisiana, where she works as a private tutor.

VIRGIL SUAREZ is the author of three books of fiction about the Cuban American experience: *Latin Jazz* (Morrow 1989, Fireside Books, 1990), *The Cutter* (Available Press/Ballantine Books, 1991), and *Welcome to the Oasis & Other Stories* (Arte Publico Press, 1992). He is the co-editor with Delia M. Poey of *Iguana Dreams: New Latino Fiction* (HarperCollins, 1992). He has completed *Havana Thursdays*, his third novel and is at work on *Sonny Manteca's Blues*, a fourth. He is also working on a book of poems and prose poems entitled *Spared Angola: Scars from a Cuban American Childhood*. He teaches in the Creative Writing Program at Florida State University. He lives in Tallahassee, Florida.

CARMEN TAFOLLA has published poetry, television screenplays, a book on Chicana women, and numerous short stories, articles, and children's works. Her latest book, *Sonnets to Human Beings and Other Selected Works by Carmen Tafolla* (Santa Monica College Press), is the first critical edition of any work by a Chicano. Her manuscripts and writings have been archived by the University of Texas Benson Latin American Collection. A native of San Antonio, she presently resides in McAllen, Texas, where she is at work on an epic novel, *La Gente*, and a movie script based on her short story "Federico y Elfiria."

DAVID UNGER was born in Guatemala and is the author of a book of poems, *Neither Caterpillar Nor Butterfly* (Es Que Somos Muy Pobres Press, New York, 1985). The poems included in this anthology are from *Watching the Rain Fly Up*, a new collection. He is also translator of Bárbara Jacob's novel *The Dead Leaves* (Curbstone Press, 1993).

GINA VALDEZ was born in Los Angeles and grew up on both sides of the U.S.-Mexican border. She has published a bilingual book of poetry, *Eating Fire* (Maize Press, 1986) and a song of the border, *Puentes y Fronteras*, 1981. Her poetry and fiction have appeared in journals and anthologies in the U.S., Mexico, and Europe. She has taught Chicana/o literature and culture at universities throughout the U.S., and is presently writing and teaching at the University of California, Los Angeles.

GLORIA VANDO's first book of poems, *Promesas: Geography of the Impossible* (Arte Publico Press, 1993) was a finalist for the 1992

Walt Whitman Award and the Poetry Society of America's Alice Fay diCastagnola Prize. A Puerto Rican, born and reared in New York City, she attended New York University. She spent her junior year at the University of Amsterdam's Tolstoy Foundation, studied painting at the Academie Julian in Paris, and traveled throughout Europe before receiving her B.A. from Texas A & M University, Corpus Christi.

E. J. VEGA was born in Oriente, Cuba, in 1961. He was educated at Brooklyn College and Columbia University, and has sailed as a deckhand on tugboats and ocean-going barges. His poetry and fiction have appeared in many literary reviews, including *Parnassus, Americas Review, Brooklyn Review, River Styx,* and *Imagine: International Chicano Poetry Journal.* Among his writing awards are the Irwin Shaw Fiction Prize, the Donald G. Whiteside Poetry award, and the Grebanier Sonnet Award. He serves on the Humanities faculty of SUNY Maritime College, Fort Schuyler, New York.

ALMA LUZ VILLANUEVA is the author of *Bloodroot, Mother, May I!* and *Life Span.* A novel, *The Ultraviolet Sky,* (Bilingual Press, 1988; Doubleday, 1993) won a 1989 Before Columbus American Book Award. She is also the author of *Naked Ladies,* a novel, and *Planet,* a book of poetry (both Bilingual Press).

TINO VILLANUEVA is from Texas but has lived on the East Coast for twenty years. His poems have appeared in *Ontario Review, Texas Quarterly, The Bloomsbury Review,* and most recently in *An Ear to the Ground: An Anthology of Contemporary American Poetry* (1989) and *After Aztlan: Latino Poets of the Nineties* (1992). His books of poetry include *Shaking Off the Dark* (1984) and *Scene from the Movie* GIANT (Curbstone, 1993). He teaches at Boston University and is editor of *Imagine: International Chicano Poetry Journal.*

RAFAEL ZEPEDA was born in 1944 in California. He has written both fiction and poetry, and his books include *By Land, Sea, and Air* (Maelstrom Press), *The Nebraska Poems* (Vergin Press), *The Yellow Ford of Texas* (Vergin Press), *The Olympic Boxing Poems* (22 Press), and *Horse Medicine and Other Stories* (Applezaba Press), which was nominated as best fiction of the year in 1992 by *The Los Angeles Times.* He teaches creative writing at California State University, Long Beach.

Acknowledgments

"Shame" by Francisco X. Alarcón, from *Snake Poems: An Aztec Invocation* by Francisco X. Alarcón, copyright © 1992 by Francisco X. Alarcón. Reprinted by permission of Chronicle Books. "L.A. Prayer" by Francisco X. Alarcón, from *No Golden Gate for Us* by Francisco X. Alarcón, copyright © 1994 by Francisco X. Alarcón. Reprinted by permission of Pennywhistle Press.

"Homecoming," "Dusting," and "Storm Windows" by Julia Alvarez, from *Homecoming*, copyright © 1984 by Julia Alvarez. Published by Dutton Signet, a division of Penguin USA, New York. Originally published by Grove Press, New York. Reprinted by permission of Susan Bergholz Literary Services.

Excerpts from "Poem VI" and from "Poem XXIII" by Jimmy Santiago Baca, from *Martín & Meditations on the South Valley*, copyright © 1986, 1987 by Jimmy Santiago Baca. Reprinted by permission of New Directions Publishing Corp.

"Leavings," "Abuelo Leopoldo Sneaks a Bite of Cream Cheese," and "For El Niño on His Arrival in the United States" by Sandra M. Castillo, from *Red Letters* by Sandra M. Castillo, copyright © 1994 by Sandra M. Castillo. Reprinted by permission of Apalachee Press.

"Pulling the Muse from the Drum" and "Herald of Cocos (I)" by Adrian Castro, copyright © 1994 by Adrian Castro. Reprinted by permission of the author.

"Morning Geography" and "Women Talk of Flowers at Dusk" by Rosemary Catacalos, copyright © 1994 by Rosemary Catacalos. Reprinted by permission of the author.

"The Poet Is Served Her Papers," "Blue Full Moon in Witch," and "From the Cables of Genocide" by Lorna Dee Cervantes, copyright © 1987 by Lorna Dee Cervantes, reprinted with permission from the publisher of *The Americas Review*, vol. 17, nos. 3 & 4, (Houston: Arte Publico Press-University of Houston, 1987).

"The Medium's Burden" and "My Grandfather's Hat" by Judith Ortiz Cofer, from *The Latin Deli: Prose and Poetry* by Judith Ortiz

239

242